GOD, WORK IT OUT

Our African Adventure

Adventures of a missionary couple who braved
venturing into Zimbabwe, Africa

"We'll go where you want us to go, Dear Lord,
O'er mountain, or plain, or sea;
We'll say what you want us to say, Dear Lord,
we'll be what You want us to be."

Don and Janet Arnett

TEACH Services, Inc.
P U B L I S H I N G
www.TEACHServices.com • (800) 367-1844

World rights reserved. This book or any portion thereof may not be copied or reproduced in any form or manner whatever, except as provided by law, without the written permission of the publisher, except by a reviewer who may quote brief passages in a review.

The author assumes full responsibility for the accuracy of all facts and quotations as cited in this book. The opinions expressed in this book are the author's personal views and interpretations, and do not necessarily reflect those of the publisher.

This book is provided with the understanding that the publisher is not engaged in giving spiritual, legal, medical, or other professional advice. If authoritative advice is needed, the reader should seek the counsel of a competent professional.

Copyright © 2019 Don and Janet Arnett
Copyright © 2019 TEACH Services, Inc.
ISBN-13: 978-1-4796-0995-6 (Paperback)
ISBN-13: 978-1-4796-0996-3 (ePub)
Library of Congress Control Number: 2018958223

All scripture quotations, unless otherwise indicated, are taken from the New King James Version®. Copyright © 1982 by Thomas Nelson. Used by permission. All rights reserved.

Scripture quotations marked NIV are taken from THE HOLY BIBLE, NEW INTERNATIONAL VERSION®, NIV® Copyright © 1973, 1978, 1984, 2011 by Biblica, Inc.® Used by permission. All rights reserved worldwide.

Published by

www.TEACHServices.com • (800) 367-1844

DEDICATION

This book is dedicated to my mother, Vera Smith. Without her help, we could not have written this book. She saved the letters that we wrote to her from Africa, which helped us to remember much of the related information.

"God Will Work It Out" is a captivating illustration of what it means to plunge into a totally unknown, unpredictable environment in response to "God's call." Once the Arnetts accept by faith the direction of the Holy Spirit, simple and forceful outcomes give evidence that God has already been at work prior to their acceptance of the call. Each section of the book is a portrait of actual happenings from the lives of real people-their varied experiences in the mission field, the impact on family left behind, and their determination to contribute to God's end-time work. The book vividly contrasts what it means to work with outdated tools and sparse supplies in contrast to the vast resources in U.S. storehouses.

Arriving during Zimbabwe's winter months, the Arnetts quickly learn the importance of depending on the advice of local missionaries, sharpening their senses concerning unfamiliar surroundings, and perfecting their methods for securing life and property-especially after they are robbed on the second night of arrival. The book contributes positively to the blending of varied methods for spreading the gospel, while interpreting cultural differences and serving the needs of the people. The importance of teamwork and comradery are sensitively portrayed.

The compact book is bursting with insight into mission life and truly gives a dramatic and emotionally enchanting account of Zimbabwe's beauty and picturesque plateaus and mountainous highlands, punctuated with great natural resources and wildlife. The reading leaves you wanting more and more. An excellent read!

—*Sandra Price, retired Professor and former Vice President of Oakwood University and Union College*

Many of us have heard missionary stories and been blessed through them, but seldom do we have an opportunity to experience the day-to-day journey of missionaries in the way Don and Janet have shared in their book, "God Will Work It Out."

As you read their reflections of the missionary time they spent in Africa, you will be transported in mind and heart to walk with them—walk with them as relief was provided to the suffering through their dental ministry—walk with them as they experienced the sadness of being apart from family and the joy of being together during return trips home and family visiting them—walk with them as they experienced the cultural practices of the area where they lived—walk with them as children were taught in a Christian School environment—walk with them as they visited games reserves and saw majestic animals in their natural habitat—walk with them as they beheld the beauty of a country few have privilege to observe—walk with them as they allowed God to "work it out."

Thank you, Don and Janet, for allowing us, through your reflections, to walk with you.

—*Pastor Dan Jarrard, ThD*

An engaging compilation of memories and events from a missionary couple's calling to serve in Africa. Follow along as they pursue greater meaning, leaving their home, family and friends, and how challenges and roadblocks would fall away as they moved forward with their work. Little details of daily life and events plant a picture of how life as a missionary in Zimbabwe strengthened their faith and changed their lives. It was a great insight into my grandparents' lives and helped me to better understand them and their faith.

—*Ryan Shea, student, University of Chicago*

TABLE OF CONTENTS

Acknowledgements . . . . *vii*
Introduction . . . . *viii*

1. How It All Began 11
2. Domestic Help. 16
3. Open Wide. 21
4. Pleasant Surprise 26
5. Hospital—Hat—Hearse 29
6. Replacement for Salina 33
7. School Daze 37
8. Beitbridge, Gateway to South Africa. 41
9. Sights Around Town .45
10. Visitors and Families Came 49
11. Spiritual Growth 52
12. "It's About Time" 56
13. Furlough Home 60
14. Grasshoppers, Slugs, Snails, and Chongololos 62
15. Unique Encounters with the Wild 67
16. Zambezi Conference .71
17. Marvelous Malawi Lake 76

18.	Solusi College	.77
19.	Fun Times	.80
20.	Victoria Falls, The Greatest Show on Earth	.83
21.	Mother Must Leave—Rules of the Country	.85
22.	Drought Woes	.87
23.	Brave Beth	.91
24.	Life in the Village	.93
25.	Seeing the Real Africa	.95
26.	Chobe National Game Park	103
27.	Hurray! Second Furlough	107
28.	Tragedy at Fairview	111
29.	Rains at Last	113
30.	Pasdad—Indian Ocean Excursion	116
31.	Better Late Than Never	119
32.	Going Home—End of Our Once-in-A-Lifetime Journey	121
33.	Remembering Zimbabwe	123
	Glossary	*125*
	News from Home	*127*

ACKNOWLEDGEMENTS

A SPECIAL THANKS to Beth Campbell for designing our book cover.

Writing this book has helped us to always remember how God did work out all our problems while missionaries in Africa, and has helped us remember all the blessings we received while working in Zimbabwe.

It has also helped to bring back memories of our fellow missionaries we worked with in Bulawayo, Zimbabwe, Africa: Ron and Dorothe Forde, Gloria and Ken Pierson, Ed and Linda Russell.

INTRODUCTION

ZIMBABWE

This former British colony for many years was known as Rhodesia named after Cecil Rhodes. However, its name changed in 1980 to Zimbabwe when civil war broke out, and Rhodesia was overthrown by Robert Mugabe and his fellow revolutionaries. The country became independent from England and took on a socialist form of government.

Zimbabwe is the second most modern country in Africa, second only to South Africa. Zimbabwe has important underground deposits of coal, tin, copper, gold, diamonds, nickel, chromium, asbestos, iron ore and lithium. The mineral wealth combined with rich farmland means Zimbabwe is a very prosperous place, much more blessed economically than most of the rest of Africa.

Zimbabwe's northern and southern borders are formed by two great rivers. The river to the north is the Zambezi. The Zambezi is 2,200 miles long and forms Zimbabwe's north and west borders. Elephants come to drink at dusk when the sun is setting, and the sky turns orange, a sight for which the Zambezi is famous. The river to the south is the Limpopo which is the international boundary between South Africa and Zimbabwe.

It is said that most people who get a taste of Africa's adventure and mystery, its wonders and surprises, carry it with them forever. It is a powerful and fascinating place.

The earliest inhabitants of Zimbabwe, as far as is known, were cave dwellers thought to be Bushmen. The two main ethnic groups are Shona and Ndebele.

Zimbabwe's Independence Day is April 18. Africa Day, May 25, is to remind everyone that, difficult as it may be, a friendly Africa working together is still a good goal.

If you think of Africa as having only thick jungles and vines, hot temperatures and dripping rainforests, you will change your mind. Africa is full of surprises. Much of Zimbabwe is high plateau and mountainous highlands. Temperatures are moderate, with little jungle heat and sunny days much of the year and nights that are cool and comfortable. Because Zimbabwe is south of the equator, its winter is in July and its summer is in December.

Zimbabwe has great forests. They don't look much different than those in North America except that Zimbabwe has no pine trees in their forests and North Americans have no baboons in their treetops!

Large-scale farming as a business was introduced by white farmers who moved to Rhodesia from South Africa at the end of the 1800s. They grew many more crops than they needed and sold their extra crops for cash. These large farms turned out to be highly successful. Zimbabwe grows maize, tobacco, tea, sugar, cotton, coffee, a variety of fruits and groundnuts (peanuts).

Rain is very important for the farmers, to say the least. When the drought comes, the rivers carry only dust, and this brings fear and hunger in all of Africa. During times of drought, all who live in the affected areas look to the skies with great concern. This is when the rain dances in the villages and prayers for rain in the churches begin.

LORD, please don't send us to Africa
Please don't send us to Africa
We don't think we've got what it takes
We're just human; we're not a Tarzan
Don't like lions, gorillas or snakes
We'll serve you here in suburbia
In our comfortable middle-class life
But please don't send us out into the bush
Where the natives are restless at night

—*Scott Wesley Brown*

1
HOW IT ALL BEGAN

DON CAME HOME from work one day and announced that he had received a letter from Ken Pierson, a missionary dentist in Bulawayo, Zimbabwe, Africa, telling him they needed another dentist to join the two dentists who were working at the Bulawayo Adventist Dental Clinic. Ken had issued a letter to former Loma Linda dental graduates.

Upon arriving home with the letter, Don asked me, "What do you think? Are you interested in going to Africa?"

Of course, I thought it was a great idea since I had already expressed interest in serving in a mission field for a year or two (not dreaming we would spend twelve years in mission work). If God could work it out, Don told Ken that we were interested.

DON'S FOLLOW UP CONTACT

We received a follow-up contact. I was asked by the General Conference of Seventh-day Adventist to work at the Adventist Dental Practice in Bulawayo, Zimbabwe. This was located on the top floor of the Better Living Center next to the Zambezi Union.

Could God work it out? Was it His will that we go? Well, there was a house and dental practice to sell; also vehicles and furniture to dispose of. But if God would work it out, we would go.

Amazingly, the first person who replied to our ad bought our house even though previous attempts to sell have failed. The doctor who bought our house said she couldn't move in for two months, the exact time we would have before we were to leave for Mission Institute in Berrien Springs, Michigan, a requirement for all missionaries to attend for three weeks. This was time well spent to teach us the ups and downs of mission life. We learned Adventist history, and how to blend in with people we are to serve. The GC sent us information on the culture and customs of Zimbabwe. Important information like Africans drive on the left side of the road, not the wrong side.

The dentist across the street from my dental office was looking for a dental practice to buy. God WAS working it out, so we felt He really did want us to accept this call from the General Conference of Seventh-day Adventists.

There was a garage sale, packing, and Janet completing her master's degree in elementary education at Alabama A & M. Then having to say goodbye to all our relatives as we made our rounds to Texas, New York, and Alabama as I waited for my Zimbabwe work permit to come.

Airplane tickets, passports, boarding passes, and our itinerary telling us what countries we will stop in. It will take two days to get there. Immunizations against cholera, hepatitis, tetanus, and typhoid were required before entering Zimbabwe. After a two month wait for my Zimbabwe work permit, we were ready to go.

The General Conference moving van came and picked up our belongings, took them to the dock, and we were on our way to Zimbabwe, Africa!

Our excited family saw us off as we boarded KLM Airlines in Dallas, Texas on September 7, 1988. Yes, Linda, it did turn out to be the adventure of our lives. Janet appreciated the beautiful corsage, Beth. Others who wished us a safe bon voyage were daughter, Debbie, her daughter, Alicia, Alex, and Jared, Linda's two boys and sister, Shirley. It was with mixed emotions leaving our family behind, but we felt God had really worked it out for us to go.

Fasten your seat belts, we are going to Africa, to the country of Zimbabwe!

You know, where all the snakes, gorillas, and lions are.

"I'll go where You want me to go, dear Lord. O'er mountain, or plain, or sea. I'll say what you want me to say, dear Lord, I'll be what You want me to be."

ARRIVAL IN SOUTH AFRICA

It is ten o'clock Monday morning—eight hours earlier than our hometown in the USA.

It's a little chilly as we leave the plane. Well, it is the middle of winter—June, July, and August are the coldest months. October, November, and December are summer months.

The Harcom brothers have gotten us a used Mercedes-Bends in excellent condition. Driving on the left side of the road with the steering wheel on the right side of the car with a stick shift isn't an easy task.

In South Africa we were picked up by Manie Harcom at the airport. He took us to his office where he introduced us to our unfamiliar car, handed me the keys and said, "Follow me; I'll take you to your motel for the night."

Five o'clock traffic, similar to USA five o'clock traffic in large cities, with driving on the unfamiliar left side of the road, was a very trying experience, to say the least. The next morning Manie took us to a grocery store to buy some things that are not available in Bulawayo.

ON TO BULAWAYO

Our trip to Bulawayo, the second largest city in Zimbabwe, was uneventful. We had the idea that we would stop at a restaurant on the Beitbridge border. Sorry, no such place. We decided to buy some food at the kiosk before starting our 200-mile journey. The only available bread is unsliced, white and unwrapped except for one band of paper in the middle. We are thankful for the peanut butter crackers and Fanta®, a popular orange soda in Africa, to wash them down.

We are arriving late this afternoon in Bulawayo where Ken and Gloria Pierson are taking us to our new home. After we unpack and put our food from South Africa in the refrigerator, we finally have time to relax after our long trip.

We are grateful for the missionaries who bring us food for our first few days. Also, they have loaned us eating and cooking utensils that we need because our shipment from the states hasn't arrived.

Many invited us to their homes. Johann and Meryl, along with their two children, Triston and Tiffany, took us to Maleme Dam, a part of Matobo Hills. We noticed a skull and cross bone sign saying NO SWIMMING— BILHARZIA.

Besides the bilharzia found in lakes and ponds, malaria and waterborne diseases exist. *Cholera has hit Zimbabwe. Not too many cases in Bulawayo; the paper said only thirty-two had died last week, so they feel the situation is better. It was bad in the refugee camps. When you read the paper, you realize where you are and what is going on in places we don't know anything about.*

The main grocery store Gloria took us to the next day compared to a down-sized Dollar General USA store. There are many shelves of canned goods with the same items on each shelf from top to bottom. No refrigerated or frozen foods are available.

Bulawayo is a city of beautiful flowers and trees lining the streets. In November and December, the blooms of the flamboyant trees follow those of the summertime jacarandas and agapanthus (African lilies) to create an appropriately red and gold Christmastime spectacular throughout the city. The beautiful poinsettia plants are spectacular being six to eight feet tall scattered throughout the city.

EARLY VISITOR—WE'VE BEEN ROBBED!

Miss Crump, one of the schoolteachers at Fairview Adventist Primary School, where I teach, offered to loan us her BIG dog, Ben, but we didn't think that was necessary. Bad mistake!

The second night we were here I woke up in the middle of the night after hearing the back door shut, and I knew something was wrong. Upon getting up, I stepped on my billfold which had been dropped on the floor, completely empty of both US and Zim currency. Janet's watch was missing along with a few clothes, including a pink dress shirt which I never wore anyway.

Checking the rest of the house, we found the jalousie windows in the living room had been carefully removed and placed on the ground. The robber had crawled in the window.

> *The second night we were here I woke up in the middle of the night after hearing the back door shut, and I knew something was wrong.*

Upon further checking, we found some of the food items we had purchased in South Africa were missing. We are sure the thief was disappointed in not finding as much as he had hoped for, as our shipment had not yet arrived from the United States. He did manage to find a big jar of peanut butter and a large bottle of olive oil among other items. These items they could sell for a large amount of money. For future protection, a neighbor carved us a knob carrier, which is similar to a police nightstick.

As a rule thieves in Zimbabwe are not violent. They will rob you, but will not kill you. They may rob you because they are hungry, or their families need food.

We quickly contacted Miss Crump and told her we were glad to take her up on her offer to borrow Ben. Actually, Big Ben was more like Gentle Ben, although he had a disliking for men.

2
DOMESTIC HELP

VERY SOON, WE started interviewing for a gardener, who would live in the kya behind our house. This would give us more security as well as the burglar bars the dental practice had installed on the windows.

Gloria helped us interview James, who turned out to be a very good domestic worker.

Shortly after the theft incident, we moved down the street to another one of the Adventist Dental Practice houses. We were happy with this new location.

Fire and Lillian were the domestic workers on this property. Soon Fire was asked to work for the Zambezi Union as their grounds maintenance worker. Lillian stayed here with us.

James helps Lillian with some of the inside housework. He washes windows and washes the car, cleans and maintains the swimming pool and he also sweeps the carpet and will until our shipment comes and brings our vacuum cleaner. Washing clothes in a tub can't be easy.

Domestic workers—Salina and James

He will be glad for our washing machine. James does gardening mostly. Besides Sabbath, he has Sunday afternoon off in order to go to his church.

The army worms have started to come to Bulawayo. They will just eat a whole garden or area of land. But the city has spray and fogging which is doing a pretty good job of keeping them under control.

Lillian stayed on until her daughter, who was baby-sitting Lillian's baby, Prince, left to go to South Africa and has not come back. That means Lillian will quit working to take care of her baby, so we have begun looking for another inside domestic worker. The government practically requires you to hire their people, so we are happy to comply.

I called Pots & Pans to see what the deal was to finding us a housemaid. I specified that I wanted one who could read a recipe and help grade simple school papers. She is to work one half a day on Sunday; no Saturdays.

We hired Evelyn; however, James isn't happy to have to share his domain with anyone. He should be glad to have some help. Evelyn is a good worker, but it wasn't long before we found out she is stealing and things are missing. We cannot trust her, so we have to let her go.

Salina, James' wife, left where she was working and came to live with James. So she is doing inside work, and now things are running smoothly at our house.

Last week we took James and his wife to Matobo Game Park. It is only thirty miles away, but they had never been there. Amazing! Their only transportation is their feet.

OUR HOUSE

Sala bononi—greetings—welcome to our house.

We moved down the street when Marvin and Beth Gotchell, the last missionaries, left on permanent return. This house is one of three houses owned by the dental practice.

Almost an acre with a six-foot rock wall, with broken glass cemented in the top, surrounds the whole yard. There is a large double iron gate with a chain lock that James locks every night. A small kopi in front with trees, rocks, and cacti make our place attractive. In the backyard there is a cactus garden. There are a hundred different kinds of cacti in Zimbabwe.

We have a double kya for domestic workers, which consists of two rooms with shower and bathroom facilities. The kya houses the gardener and inside domestic help.

Trees in our yard are peach, apricot, mulberry, passion fruit and paw paw (papaya). James has his own garden.

We noticed a family of lemurs that look like squirrels except for their big ears and big eyes. Their tails are long and skinny with hair on the very end of their tails. They are capable of jumping long distances from limb to limb. They are nocturnal, so you see them only around dusk. They play around in the trees; you never see them on the ground.

Our yard is brightened by a great variety of trees. There are two lovely reddish-orange African tulip trees and another huge yellow tree. A yesterday—today—and tomorrow bush gives us enjoyment for three consecutive days. This lovely bush blooms several times during the year.

Bougainvillea, hibiscus, bird of paradise, roses, several ferns, and a three-foot jade plant make our yard attractive.

We have a mixture of huge pink and blue hydrangea bushes in our front yard. Because some have been getting soapy water, they have turned blue.

We have an exotic large white flower, called the Night Blooming Cereus that blooms only one day and one night each year.

Inside our house, beautiful African violets are blooming continuously.

The white frog on our front porch that changes color, like a chameleon, is an extra delight. James is afraid of chameleons, calling them evil.

We are thankful for James who takes care of our vegetable garden. He is growing corn, cucumbers, a few green beans, lettuce, tomatoes, and squash.

DOGS

Both Terry, the terrier, and Rocky, the boxer, we inherited from Marvin and Beth when they left PR. We have grown fond of Big Ben, but it is time to return Ben to Miss Crump. And we understand why Miss Crump wants him back.

2. DOMESTIC HELP ✛ 19

Night Blooming Cereus

Terry loves to climb trees and our six-foot wall. His absence makes Rocky very unhappy and he barks and barks when Terry is gone. The neighbor called one morning about 3 am and asked us, "Are you aware that your dog is barking?" It is time to find Rocky a new home where he will get all the attention he needs.

However, we do need a good watchdog.

"Let's go investigate the ad in the paper for a Rottweiler puppy. They are known for making excellent watchdogs."

As soon as we saw the pup, we fell in love with him. He is seven weeks old and weighs 20 pounds. All the way home he behaved himself while Janet held him on her lap.

DJ, the name we chose for our Rottweiler, didn't take long to get big enough to play the part of a good watchdog. DJ is not the typical Rottweiler;

he is gentle and playful. Most of the schoolchildren like him when they come over to our house for school activities. There are two people DJ does not like, however. One is the veterinarian; we can understand that, and the other is Ed. We cannot figure out why he growls and picks on Ed.

Janet and I just finished dipping the dogs; ticks have been bad this year, but thankfully the fleas haven't been so bad.

DJ did well at the Rottweiler Club Obedience Training School. When it was over the trainer offered to train him as an attack dog for our own benefit. Of course, we declined the offer. We like DJ just the way he is.

SNAKES

One evening we heard Terry barking his head off, and he would not stop. We looked out at the cactus garden and saw this fairly large Egyptian cobra swaying back and forth. He was raised up about eighteen inches and hissing at Terry. We called the police, but by the time they got there with a blunderbuss shotgun, the cobra had left. We never saw it again. After about two hours Terry quit barking.

James, our gardener, killed a Mozambique spitting cobra. Janet took it to school for the children to identify, and it was a Mozambique spitting cobra. Other than a Green Mamba we saw in a tree when we first moved into this house, we saw no more snakes.

3
OPEN WIDE

MISSIONARIES ARE SENT to help prepare foreign nationals to eventually manage their own local church affairs. One of the government stipulations on my work permit was for me to train nationals to do my job.

Our well-equipped three-chair facility at the Bulawayo Adventist Dental Clinic was as modern as any facility would be in the United States. Four national Zimbabweans helped run the clinic. Zimbabwe lab technicians make dentures and partials.

We had a receptionist and three dental assistants as well as Drs. Ken Pierson, Marvin Gotchell, and myself. Drs. Ed Russell, Ron Forde, and Bill Taylor also served as dentists during our seven-year stay. Patients came from Mozambique, Zambia, and Botswana as well as Zimbabwe.

We are known as a self-supporting dental clinic, but our salaries come from our General Conference. Our furloughs and insurance are paid for by the General Conference. The monies generated by the clinic go back to the General Conference as a reimbursement for the dental missionary expenses. Therefore, we support ourselves, but we are employees of the General Conference of Seventh-day Adventists.

Our dental clinic sponsored one national Zimbabwean in dental school in South Africa, who has plans for returning to be of missionary service. Some of our other medical institutions are now staffed by nationals, who received training sponsored by our health institutions that are funded by the General Conference of Seventh-day Adventists.

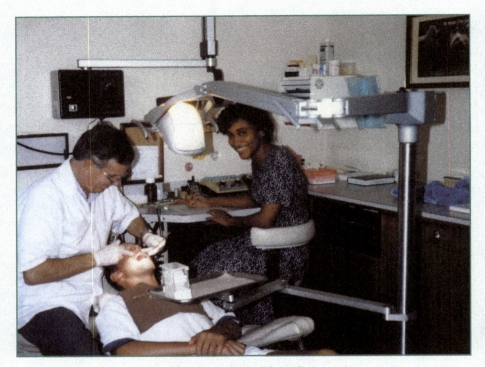

Don and his assistant with a clinic patient

Harare, the capital of Zimbabwe, is where I had to go in person to register with the dental board before I could obtain a Zimbabwe dental license or begin to work in the dental clinic.

Barry Krouse, a dental student from Loma Linda, rode his bike to work almost every day. He lived at Solusi College with his parents for eight years and spent five years in Kenya with his missionary parents before he attended Loma Linda School of Dentistry in Loma Linda, California. When he arrived, we gave him a surprise birthday party.

A few problems are to be expected at working in a third-world country. One problem we had was embezzlement and theft by our employees. Another was that very few people use deodorant so we had to reeducate our noses to tolerate the BO.

One patient had been a guide on the Zambezi River. On one excursion the boat tipped over and a hippopotamus severed his leg above the knee. The most dangerous animal in Africa is the hippo.

I went to the office this morning and took apart one of our amalgam mixers. It had stopped working and we definitely need it. It seems some solder joints on the electronic control board have broken loose. I will have to find a soldering iron and some solder and maybe it can be fixed. While there I took another old amalgamator apart to see if it could be fixed. It will take a lot of work to get it working in good order but I think it can be fixed. Remember, this is Africa. Things are not as available here as in the United States.

The Better Living Center's five-day stop smoking plan, downstairs from the dental practice, is an asset to the community.

The Better Living Center is conducting vegetarian cooking classes. Linda Russell, Dr. Russell's wife, is helping with them. It will run four consecutive Sundays. Also the four next Mondays another class will begin.

One of my jobs at the dental office is to order dental supplies. One morning Linda and Janet took Ed and me with four empty suitcases to the Bulawayo airport to fly to Harare. We are to look over some dental supplies that we may be able to use from a dentist who is selling out his practice.

Better Living Center and dental clinic

It's Sunday morning and someone just showed up at our front gate. He is from Gweru, about 100 miles away, and said he hadn't slept for three nights. I will take him to the dental clinic, as he needs a tooth extracted. We have emergency patients like this often.

I was asked to treat an AIDs patient in her home. My assistant and I took precautionary measures, and extracted a tooth for the lady.

PASDAD

Pan Africa Seventh-day Adventist Dentists

It wasn't long after we arrived in Bulawayo that we went to the Seventh-day Adventist dental convention. To maintain our US dental state license, continuing education is mandatory.

The SDA Dental Convention, for all dentists in Africa, was held at Kariba Dam, Zimbabwe. Eleven other dentists and myself earned twenty hours of instruction by two Loma Linda dentists.

Kariba Dam is the largest of 7,000 dams in Zimbabwe. It took us eight hours to drive to the convention where we also enjoyed the Kariba game park.

We took a tour boat ride to Fothergill Island where we ate lunch. Afterwards we went to the island on an exciting game safari ride where we saw some big elephants, Cape buffalo, impala, zebra, and birds.

While we were on Lake Kariba, we saw hippopotamuses and crocodiles. The lake had bilharzia, so we chose not to swim in it. However, ten miles out we were told it was safe from bilharzia, crocks, and hippos. Some of our group jumped off the top deck of the boat to enjoy a swim.

Upon returning, we ate dinner at the hotel outside under the mango trees. There were several mango trees near the lodge. They are delicious, but not good for Janet. She is allergic to mango skin and ended up with mango poisoning.

My face was swollen mostly around my eyes. Thankfully I got a shot yesterday from our nurse neighbor, Gloria. It seemed to help the swelling, but when I woke up this morning the swelling around one eye was worse, so Don called the pharmacy and drove downtown to pick up an Rx. I had tried to be careful knowing mango skin is not my friend, even though I have no trouble eating the fruit. Well, some boys were throwing the mangoes down from the tree, and I caught a couple to take to our room. I washed my hands and face GOOD, I thought. Maybe the soap doesn't work here.

Two dental instructors came and talked to us dentists' wives with interesting information and helpful instructions. These Loma Linda ladies brought us goodie bags and crafts to do. These things we can't get in Africa.

4
PLEASANT SURPRISE

SHORTLY AFTER WE arrived home from our first PASDAD, we had a pleasant surprise.

After three months, we got notice that our shipment from the United States has landed in Bulawayo. Yes, the day has arrived! Our shipment is here in the front yard of our house. A huge twenty-foot blue container—locked until Sunday morning.

It took all day—from 8:00 a.m. to 6:15 p.m. to get the container delivered and unloaded from the depot to our house. It was interesting to watch the crane lift it from the flatbed of the truck. The truck driver took fifty-five minutes to drive it here. He followed us so he wouldn't get lost. The container weighs 10,700 pounds. It is a fifteen-minute drive normally.

I will have to go down to the customs department and bring a customs officer to the "grand opening" so she can inspect the goods we are bringing into the country. We will have to get the lady at 7:00 a.m.—on our request so we can get started early unpacking.

HOME IMPROVEMENT

New carpet was installed, kitchen painted yellow (Janet's favorite color), and the kitchen door moved for better access to the back porch. Also, our house was painted outside.

Our driveway got a facelift. About ten men worked on our driveway laying stones in cement. With all those men working on it and with someone to supervise them they got it done pretty fast. It was a very nice outcome. Labor in Zimbabwe is cheap and products are high. The opposite of America where the labor is expensive and the products not as much.

James was happy to have a washing machine, but he preferred to hang the clothes on the clothesline than use the clothes dryer. Salina appreciated the vacuum cleaner. However, all our possessions did not make it on the first shipment. We had to wait patiently for the next time around. A shipment of books for Solusi College and Fairview School were included. Also, a few empty boxes were on our container to fill in space. Step-down transformers 220 to 115 are a must here.

TWO MONTHS LATER

FINAL SHIPMENT ARRIVES

Hurray!!! This is the day. Don has gone to the dental practice to meet with the customs officer, who will check our shipment. The container is there in the parking lot. Ed has gone to pick up the customs officer and take him to the ADP. The key Ed had didn't work. Either the Atlantic Ocean water corroded the lock, or someone tried to open it and jammed it. But they have a hacksaw in case the key won't work. Ed and Don are determined to get that shipment unloaded today! We have lots of domestic help also.

Our bikes and ping pong table arrived with our second shipment, so we got a little exercise. The shipment came in time for Christmas. December is summer time here. Zimbabweans don't recognize a spring or fall season. After summer is winter, then summer again.

Christmas isn't as commercialized in Zimbabwe as it is in the States. Even the radio stations wait until December before they play Christmas music. Then they play Christmas music only about every tenth song.

A typical African Christmas is when the kids swim in Russells' swimming pool. The Russells have two girls, Shila and Amy. Fordes have three children, Shana, Tony, and Kim. Piersons have two boys, Kenny and Jeremy.

Boxing day, Whitsunday, is the day after Christmas. The tradition is to hand a Christmas box of left-over goodies to the mail carrier, newspaper carrier, or any delivery person.

5
HOSPITAL—HAT—HEARSE

WELL, AFTER THREE weeks Salina is still in the hospital. The hospital called James this morning and said they were transferring her to another hospital. She may get better care there. The hospitals are very poor quality. It is hard to see anything done for the patient. The wards have about thirty beds and are old. It's hard to believe the conditions that exist.

THREE WEEKS LATER

SAD NEWS

James' wife died after three weeks in the hospital. The whole family and friends get together to mourn for five or more days, comfort one another, plan for the funeral and eat. They usually have one main place where they all meet, and this time it was Salina's brother's house. But James also had people coming to his kya all through the day to show their sympathy. For three nights they sang and prayed and sometimes they listened to someone speak. There have been as many as forty people gathered in and around James' kya.

We had to try to find out our responsibilities. It seemed we were expected to help by purchasing some maize (cornmeal for sadza—their main staple) to help feed the relatives. Also, they needed help on some of the funeral expenses. Don helped James with transportation, also.

Salina's gravesite

While Don had appointments booked at the dental clinic, I attended Salina's funeral. Funerals are conducted quite differently than the US. When I took Esther, Russells' domestic worker with me, the funeral home attendants were waiting outside for the family members to go in first. Someone directed me to the door and told me to go in. It was a small room with about forty chairs, but when the place started to fill up, the women started to sit on the floor.

In Africa the women sit on one side of the parlor; men on the other. Well, I took a seat in the back, but they came and told me to sit up front. It reminded me of the parable Jesus told: "When you are invited, go and sit in the lowest place, so that when your host comes, he may tell you, 'Friend, move up higher.' Then you will be honored" (Luke 14:10, NIV).

WHAT! NO HAT?

By the way, I was the only woman who didn't have a head covering, the only woman who had hose on, and the only woman who was white. I did wear a black dress, but Mrs. Mlingo forgot to tell me about the hat. However, since I am not from their country, they didn't seem to mind. In fact, they treated me like I was someone special. There was singing, prayer, and a very short speech, all in Ndebele. Before the service, some ladies brought bougainvillea flowers they had picked and made into small sprays. Unfortunately, the flowers had died. They had messages written on the flowers which someone read later at the gravesite. Well, we all filed by the casket—box, they call it. The box was inside what looked like a marble casket. Two candles were burning. You could see only Salina's face. There were white cloths about her head and face.

After the service, the people loaded up the bus the family had hired. It was packed. Salina's mother came from Lupine. She had a cane, couldn't see well, and had no shoes on. It looked as if there was not a place for her to ride on the bus to the grave, as the bus was full. However, there was a station wagon she rode in. Then James was looking around for places for people to ride. He didn't even have a ride, so you know what happened. I took a truckload and forgot about school. I didn't have a choice. I wasn't planning to stay for the graveside service, but I was thankful for Linda Russell who was teaching my students for me at school. I knew the funeral would be long.

It was quite a ways to the grave. There were five vehicles all full. The bus and the hearse, which Salina's daughter and others rode in were full. There was no room for James if he had wanted to ride. Why James seemed to be in the background was probably because Salina was his second wife. His first wife died also, and he had no children by her. We got to the grave and unloaded. We all walked behind the hearse for a ways, and the people sang hymns in Ndebele. A canopy was over the grave. The graves are very close together. Who do you think carried the casket to the grave? Six women. The women are the pallbearers who carry the casket from the funeral home to the gravesite, but a couple of men helped when it seemed too heavy. Most everyone walks behind the casket, so I did, too. At the grave site there were several speeches.

Esther interpreted for me a little of what they were saying. She said they were asking me to come up and say a few words on Salina's behalf since I was her madam. Nobody told me I would be asked to speak. What should I say? I did go up and said a few words that God must have given me. Of course, I said she was a good worker, and I had the cleanest windows in town. I'm sure half of the 200 people couldn't understand me. But the men tried to translate what I said. They appreciated that I was there.

The funeral is followed by a meal for everyone. All outdoors, of course. They buried Salina's shoes and a bowl with her. They also buried something else of hers in the dirt, but I couldn't make out what it was.

They had a pot of dirt that different members of the family took turns sprinkling over the casket. We walked back to the vehicle and saw even more people going to the son's house. James said it was a custom to wash our hands after a funeral. There was a BIG tub of water outside the son's house with a bunch of leaves in it, but we all washed our hands, and some put some water on the bottoms of their shoes. All the people got on the bus and left. There was a long line waiting to get inside the small house and very small yard. It was time to eat. Now it was time for me to leave. I took some who lived in our neighborhood back through town and made stops close to where they worked or lived. I'm glad I went to the whole thing. An experience I may never have the opportunity to witness again. My being there was evidently important to James. I wouldn't have missed this day in Africa for the world.

James seemed to be doing well after the funeral. He worked inside and outside of the house. He washed the truck and tended the garden. He seemed to be doing alright since Salina died. He got his hair shaved, although not bald, just really short. It is a custom for the family men to do that when someone has died. Some wear a black band on their upper arm. I understand women wear black for a whole year if their husband dies. If one of their children dies, they wear black for six months. Or if they don't wear black, they wear their clothes inside out. It could be a black sweater every day for six months.

6
REPLACEMENT FOR SALINA

TITSI REPLACED SALINA. Titsi believes that James killed his wife. However, no proof; just a suspicion of another African worker.

We've been taking Titsi to the youth meetings and to church. She enjoys going and says she now has new friends.

One Friday night Titsi gave us a fright. Being winter, she built a fire in a pan (a big cut-off metal container), and after it stopped smoking she took it into her room and shut the windows and door. Needless to say, she was overcome by a lack of oxygen. James and a friend just happened to hear her fall. They managed to get her outside and then alerted us. We took her to the hospital, and they gave her oxygen and valium to calm her down. About an hour later, we brought her home. I didn't think she would try that again.

It really did scare us when James came knocking on our bedroom window. We got dressed in a hurry and rushed out to see Tstsi laying on the ground.

It really did scare us when James came knocking on our bedroom window. We got dressed in a hurry and rushed out to see Tstsi laying on the ground. They were cooling her off with wet towels. She didn't remember anything until she was in the emergency room. Some who do such foolish things never survive to tell about it. James said there are a lot of reports of such incidences. She said later she now has enough blankets. She didn't have on the knee socks I gave her, so her feet were very cold. She had a nice warm suit she wears in the winter, and she did have that on.

THE WEATHER REPORT

The weather can get quite cold in the winter months of July and August. James built a good fire in the fireplace tonight. There are no heating systems in the houses, but we can always get warm with the car heater or with the electric blanket. The space heaters are very helpful at home and at school also.

BIG TROUBLE

One day Janet and I had to have a talk with our domestic workers. Titsi and James had been at each other for about a week and seemed to be having a hard time getting along. The age difference and different tribes made conflicts. At first, they got along well—they both went to cooking classes together. But that was one of the problems. James said Africans eat sadza, not rice, when Titsi wanted to cook rice. Being a typical African, he wasn't into changes.

James had been with us four and a half years at this point, and he thought he owned the domestic quarters. He may have been a little envious since Titsi got to work inside and he had to work outside. He was also jealous because we took Titsi to church. He told her she should not join our church.

James gave Titsi such a hard time she refused to live in the kya and moved out to stay with a friend down the street. She said that in a month she would move back to her sister's in town. We were not happy with the situation.

We did not give James Titse's room in the kya and told him we were going to use it for storage. We were not happy with his attitude. I sent him a letter giving him guidelines, as he was getting out of hand.

James also tried to scare Titsi into leaving. The Africans are very superstitious, and it doesn't take much to scare them. James told Titsi she would die here in her kya; that his wife died here, and one man died here also. Of course, he failed to mention that they both died in the hospital. Titse has been very cautious sprinkling salt and urine around the walls of her room to keep the evil spirits away.

SATANIC FORCES

Sandra was a lovely sixteen-year-old girl who was a member of our Bulawayo church. She was a very enthusiastic girl who loved to witness about Jesus to her non-Christian friends where she attended one of the local high schools. This was not an Adventist school, so many students are from different denominations, including some who claim to be Satan worshipers. One day when Sandra was witnessing about Jesus, she was confronted by three of her classmates who are members of a satanic cult. Ridiculing her and not accepting her beliefs they told Sandra, "Satan is looking for girls like you, and you will be hearing from him."

This curse turned out to be real. A couple of days later, Sandra started to act strangely, so the school called her parents, and they took her to the doctor. He couldn't find anything wrong with her. She was having difficulty speaking and having body contortions. Unfortunately, she was being harassed by a satanic spirit. It happened at school and then continued at home whenever she prayed or mentioned the name of Jesus. She would go into contortions and couldn't speak. Her eyes seemed to bulge out, her neck bowed, her mouth was drawn open, and her tongue sometimes protruded. About twenty ministers, elders, and others were continually praying with her. She was fine as long as there are no prayers or mention of spiritual things.

The elders and deacons were called to Sandra's house to pray for Sandra. After some songs were sung, we all knelt and offered prayers as we all held hands. It was a very touching scene. The songs and prayers went on for about two and a half hours. After that the young girl seemed to be totally exhausted. The contortions came slower. The parents then put her to bed, and most of the people left. We returned home, and around midnight the telephone rang. Sandra's father was calling to let us know that Sandra has returned to her normal self. I knew it was Mr. Moyo telling us the good news. After four days Jesus was the victor, and the evil spirit had left Sandra. She has not been bothered since and is still witnessing.

All across Africa laws against witchcraft remain in force. Of course, most witch doctors choose to be called traditional healers, who sometimes mix up potions that make their patients sicker. Others use the power of superstition to squeeze money from the poor and those ready to believe. Zimbabwe's association of traditional healers boasts 24,000 members, whereas the health ministry's doctors, nurses, and junior workers boast 11,000. Modern doctors are respected for relieving symptoms, but many Africans believe that diseases have spiritual roots and require a healer in touch with spirits. These spirit mediums can cast spells, get in touch with disgruntled spirits that bring troubles like infertility, disrespectful children, and even business failures. Some businessmen go to the witch doctors to seek evil spells to be cast on their competitors. Cases have occurred that involved killing of young children to obtain body parts used to mix magic potions. So long as Africans believe in these spirits, the influence of the witch doctors and mediums will remain. In some cases even professed SDAs will, as a last resort, go to a traditional healer.

The Zimbabwean government has encouraged the foundation of the Traditional Healers Association. By this means the government has attempted to exercise some control over them, even to the point of offering them some rudimental medical training such as treatment of diarrhea and control of AIDS. Also by encouraging the use of their razor blades on only one patient and then disposing of the used blade.

Few inroads are being made into converting witch doctors, but Dr. Forde, one of the dentists from our Adventist Dental Clinic, witnessed the burning and burial of a witch doctor's paraphernalia when he was converted to Christianity. The ADP is now the sponsor of the witch doctor's son. He is today attending Solusi University studying ministry and planning to return to his tribal area to preach the good news.

7
SCHOOL DAZE

Fairview Adventist Primary School is where I spend much time teaching third, fourth, and fifth grades. They are wonderful, well-behaved children from different denominations and backgrounds: Seventh-day Adventists, Catholics, other Christians, and two Hindu children attend our school. This brother and sister have a live-in god who lives in their home as a guardian. He predicted that the girl, Janika, would be a doctor and her brother, Shante, would die before age 21. Genevive Mlingo is our

Fairview Adventist School

headmistress. She, Dorothy Forde, Dr. Forde's wife from the US, and I are teachers for grades one through eight.

SCHOOL ACTIVITIES

To begin the day, we have morning lineup where children are required to wear their neat school uniforms. The children in all schools—primary, secondary, high school, and college—wear school uniforms.

Morning exercises on the playground may include jumping jacks or marching. Worship and singing in our classroom is a priority. Prayer bands are conducted weekly.

Zimbabwe primary schools follow the regular school curriculum including English, math, history, social studies, reading, spelling, art, and the local traditional language, Ndebele. It is required that Ndebele or Shona be taught in all primary schools. Of course, I am not qualified to teach Ndebele even though I have taken a course in basic Ndebele. To prove it, I have a certificate of attendance for a beginning basic five-week course. And that is what I did, attended class, and found out I am not a linguist. The Ndebele have an interesting click which is really tricky to add to their language.

Ndebele is spoken as a second language in Bulawayo and the southern part of Zimbabwe. Shona, spoken by 85% of the population, is spoken as a second language in Harare and the northern part of Zimbabwe. English is the official language of Zimbabwe and is spoken by all whites and most educated blacks. In the rural areas, however, most of the people do not understand English and converse in their native tongue.

The government syllabus allows schools to have a religious and moral teaching. In fact, they require it. Our books fulfill these requirements all except Buddhism, Mohammedism, and Hinduism. School supplies are scarce. They each have one workbook for all subjects.

Soccer is lots of fun at recess. Tuesday and Thursday afternoons the kids would pile into my truck, and we would head for the swimming pool where they took swimming lessons at the Bulawayo swimming pool.

I was very leery about driving in Africa. It was really scary driving in Bulawayo with the traffic on the opposite side of the road that we Americans are used to, as well as the steering wheel and shift on the right side of the car. Just riding in the car was nerve-racking. I finally got up enough courage to venture out in the traffic. We made many field trips to nearby educational sites.

FIELD TRIPS

KAMI RUINS

Kami Ruins is an ancient dwelling city where people lived and worshipped many years ago. Mr. Payne, a helper with the children, and I took the fifth and sixth grades to this old walled village for our Bible class. The children spotted a deadly black mamba snake in a tree.

The black mamba is one of the world's deadliest snakes. It is the fastest land snake in the world, the longest species of venomous snakes in Africa, and the second longest in the world. Their venom is potentially lethal. Two drops of venom will kill you.

NATURAL HISTORY MUSEUM

We had been studying about heaven and the New Jerusalem in our Bible class. One day I took the fourth and fifth graders to the Natural History Museum to look for the twelve gemstones in the twelve foundations of New Jerusalem. I couldn't get all twenty students in the truck so had to take two trips or get someone to chauffeur part of them. The History Museum is located in Centennial Park in downtown Bulawayo.

What a wonderful place to learn, study, and observe. We searched for the twelve gemstones found in Revelation 21. The different colors of the stones are beautiful: jasper, sapphire, chalcedony, emerald, sardonyx, carnelian, chrysolite, topaz, chrysoprase, jacinth, and amethyst. We found just about all of them.

CHIPANGALI WILDLIFE ORPHANAGE

Chipangali is not a zoo or a game park, but rather a haven for wild animals which have little hope for survival in the wild—creatures which have been orphaned, abandoned, injured, born in captivity, or brought up unsuccessfully as pets.

Chipangali is where, when possible, rescued animals and birds are rehabilitated and returned to the wild. If safe release into their natural habitat is not possible, animals are cared for and kept for educational purposes and study.

The children love visiting this wildlife orphanage. There are lions, cheetah, rhinoceros, snakes, leopards, zebras, and many birds. Being able to pet some of them is a special treat.

8
BEITBRIDGE, GATEWAY TO SOUTH AFRICA

WE GOT NOTICE that our Toyota pick-up truck had been shipped by boat from Japan to South Africa. We were allowed to bring two vehicles duty-free into Zimbabwe. Johan Seligman drove us to pick up our truck. The customs officer gave us a very hard time and refused to let us bring our truck into Zimbabwe until we could provide additional paperwork.

Since Johan was staying in Johannesburg, we called Gloria Pierson to come and rescue us. Her six-hour drive one way was very much appreciated. Then we were on our way for the second time to Beitbridge to collect (that's Zim language for pick up) our truck.

We were back in the same place, talking to the same customs officer who gave us such a hard time before when we came to get our truck. We had all the information they asked for: papers, canceled checks, dates when the truck was ordered, bank statement, and other things he required for us to have.

He was beginning to give us a hard time again. After two hours and twenty-five minutes, he finally left the room, and now it was time to pray earnestly to soften this customs officer's heart, as he is determined not to let us have our truck. God would have to work it out, as it seemed that was

God would have to work it out, as it seemed that was the only solution to our problem.

the only solution to our problem. He came in, and we saw him filling out the paperwork and finally said we could have our truck. He also informed us that they would be watching us to make sure Janet was the only one driving it since it was in her name. He made it clear that there is to be no church work done using this truck.

Shifting the truck is more complicated than the car, so I drove the truck out of the parking area. We stopped by a baobab tree to eat our lunch and thank God for working it out. This strange looking tree looks as if it was planted upside down. In the winter time as its branches look like roots sticking up.

On our six-hour trip home we stopped at the Tshipise mineral baths, at the northern Transvaal hotel.

EYE WITNESS TO CRIME

Later we drove with Johann and Meryl to South Africa to buy groceries we could not buy in Zimbabwe; mostly tropical fruit, nuts, juices, and olive oil, among other things, and to pick up our new green diesel Pajero made by Mitsubishi.

While waiting in our room, I looked out the window of our second-floor hotel room and just happened to see a young man trying to open a car door. He was crouched down, so that is what made me suspicious. Well, he quickly opened the door, grabbed a portable radio from the front of the car, shut the door, and ran crouched down toward a waiting car. We could see the whole thing as plain as day. The car door was already opened, so he got in really fast and took off. I called Don to come to the window. He is better at remembering details than I am. So he could identify the car, which had stripes on the fender.

The man was around twenty years old, had on dark shorts, light pullover shirt, and sandals. He had very dark hair, was well tanned, and small build. We didn't see him smash the window, but we saw afterward he did break the glass. We wrote a statement for the police and took it to the manager.

My eyewitness report submitted to the manager of City Lodge:

Approximately at 3:45 p.m., 15 January 1992, I witnessed a man force entry into a white automobile located in the parking area of City Lodge. The man looked to be in his early 20s. He was white, well-tanned, very dark wavy (or curly) hair. He was small built, around 5' 9". Wearing a dark pair of shorts and light pullover shirt. After opening the left front door, he removed something from the car that seemed to be the size of a radio. After leaving the car, he ran crouched down to the right side of a two-door waiting car with a female passenger besides the male driver who appeared to be in his 20s. The car was older and was reddish brown in color. On the right side of the car three or four vertical stripes that followed the slope of the back fender and were darker in color.

This is so common a sight that I doubt there was any follow-up on this incident.

SCAMMED

Not until it was over, did I realize the kid duped me. I was in the car stopped, and this boy showed up on his bicycle. He let me think I had hit him. Of course, I was apologetic, but he said he wasn't hurt. I asked him how much he wanted. He named some large amount. I had only $20.00 with me, so I said I would have to go get the rest. He said, "Oh, that's alright." He was happy for the $20.00. Then I knew he was a fake. "Live and learn," they say.

Other instances—sometimes people would come to the school and ask for money so they could take a bus to get to a distant town saying their mother had died, and they needed to get to the funeral. It's strange how many mothers died, but that seems to be the most popular line.

Even the Zambezi Union got taken one time. The man came by the office, signed papers, and was trusted to pay back the money. I think he also got a new suit. Nobody ever heard from him again.

One man asked us to loan him money until the next morning. He had a good story. Said he worked for the government and wouldn't get paid until the next day. But he needed money to buy food for his family. He said his son would come by our church the next morning and give us the money. Of course, you don't loan anyone money; you just give it as a donation if you see the need, and don't expect to ever see it again.

9
SIGHTS AROUND TOWN

QUEEN ELIZABETH COMES TO BULAWAYO

Queen Elizabeth and Prince Philip arrived in Bulawayo yesterday. Thousands of people lined the streets to see the queen. It was a big thing for Bulawayo. They didn't mind waiting in the rain. We watched it on TV. Dawn, one lady from our church, went downtown and waited a long time to have her picture taken with the queen.

THE STREET MARKET

Fife Street market—baskets, fresh cut flowers, paintings, tablecloths, doilies, and macramé were a few of the beautiful crafts we liked. Animal figurines carved out of wood or soapstone were plentiful. If you go downtown early, you could see women sitting on the sidewalk making baskets and doilies. Carvings from one piece of wood are unbelievable. Pictures are made from banana skins. African craftsman are very talented when it comes to wood and stone carvings.

Sandellas, a downtown store, is a favorite place to shop. We bought souvenirs made of mahogany, ebony, soapstone, malachite, and verdite. Verdite is a beautiful green gemstone found only in Zimbabwe and South Africa. Serpentine is a black stone, more common and pretty, but not as expensive. There is no ban on ivory yet, so we bought a few items of ivory.

Bulawayo street market

We purchased gifts for our family. The ostrich eggs were a favorite. A hand crocheted dress for granddaughter Alicia fit perfectly. Pocket knives with ivory handles for the sons-in-law. Peg solitaire board games with semi-precious stone marbles, baskets, tablecloths, and doilies were popular items. Jared and Alex, our grandsons, liked the drums we sent them.

Dr. Baker gave the street market vendor a US twenty-dollar bill. That was enough for a month's salary. Happy day for the vendor.

If you want to buy anything you will use Zim money. It is very pretty with different colors on different denomination bills. The largest bill is twenty dollars. The bills and coins all have the image of the great legendary Zimbabwe bird.

CURRENCY

We could apply for our holiday allowance. It isn't much, but it was a way for us to convert some Zimbabwe dollars into US currency. It is quite a process to apply and then return to the bank two weeks later to have the traveler's checks issued. No other country is willing to exchange Zimbabwe dollars for their own country's dollars.

DRESS—CLOTHES—ATTIRE

On the street and in churches we saw people's dress is similar to our dress in the States. The ladies wear dresses. Men dress casually, except for church and business meetings, when all the men wear suits and ties. Everybody dresses up for church, funerals, and weddings.

TRANSPORTATION AROUND TOWN

Peugeot station wagons and emergency taxis carry passengers all over town. They are so jammed full, I could see the passengers hanging out the back of them. I took a taxi home to get another key because we had locked our key in the truck. By the time I got back, Don had gotten a small boy to climb in the back window to unlock the door.

The most popular form of transportation is the bus. Passengers are piled high. When they move they pile their furniture, boxes, animals, and all their belongings on top of the bus. Mostly everyone uses their feet for transportation.

THE NATIONAL HISTORY MUSEUM OF ZIMBABWE

This outstanding museum came about in 1901. It houses all the natural sciences departments catered by the organization. Departments in mammalogy with a collection of 75,000 specimens, ornithology, 90,000 study skins, 1,000 skeletons, 5,000 clutches of eggs, and 150 nests. Herpetology, 1,000 specimens, ichthyology collection over 50,000 specimens, invertebrates, over 5,000 specimen lots. We were fortunate to have this Natural History Museum in Bulawayo. It is a great place for looking and learning. Surrounding the museum are flamboyant (Poinciana), jacaranda, bougainvillea, trees of poor man's orchid, and poinsettia trees some as tall as 15–20 feet. The History Museum is next to the Bulawayo City Park.

TRADE FAIR

The Trade Fair comes once a year to Bulawayo. We enjoyed drums and marimba music while a few men danced and sang an African tune while we shopped. It is quite an art for a mother who put her baby on her back. It's probably not as easy as it looks, but this mother had no trouble. Mothers carry their babies on their backs wherever they go; even while balancing a heavy basket on their heads.

Several things were brought into the trade fair from South Africa; tractors, farming equipment, appliances, furniture or anything they could barter or trade for.

10

VISITORS AND FAMILIES CAME

FOUR PEOPLE CAME from Alabama. Joyce Knight, long-time friend we met in Birmingham, and with her, she brought Gerald Martin and Richard Hallock, the president of the Gulf States Conference. They came to see what the needs are in Africa and to promote missions when they go back to the states. Don drove them to Matobo Game Park to see a few animals. Joyce so generously gave us a large jar of much-appreciated coins she had been saving to buy supplies for our school children.

Paula and Wayne

Daughter Paula and husband Wayne came from Alabama to see us and to see Africa. We saw many animals, but NO elephants. Paula began to wonder if there are really 120,000 elephants in Zimbabwe. She saw a lion and his kill. Didn't see the kill, but the cape buffalo was lying there with the lion close by. The lion wasn't about to let anything or anybody near it. We went back three times, and he was still there close by, but it didn't look as if he had eaten any of the buffalo.

We all saw the usual—giraffe, impala, zebra, sable, waterbuck, and kudu, Zimbabwe's national animal. And some not so common, like the bat-eared fox, black-backed jackal, and side-striped jackal. At Matobo Game Park we saw several rhinos among other animals.

Paula and Wayne had an enjoyable time at Victoria Falls even though they got wet from the spray. Because the wind was blowing the wrong way, we really got the spray. Victoria Falls is twice as deep and at least twice as wide as Niagara Falls. Paula and Wayne went on the 'flight of the angels', a small plane ride which took them over the falls. We had enjoyed the flight previously.

We met a herd of goats on the road when coming home, but no problem. We just waited patiently until they crossed the road.

SAFARI WITH BAKERS—DENA SAFARI LODGE

We were happy to have Grace and J. Baker visit us for two months. Dr. J relieved Dr. Forde while he went on furlough, and Grace helped out at Fairview School teaching third-grade reading. Of course, they and we enjoyed going on a safari while they were here.

On our safari trip, we saw a beautiful leopard. It was at night, but the guide had a bright light directed at the leopard. Bright enough so we hoped the pictures would come out. The only trouble was us freezing in the open safari truck late that night and early in the morning. We stayed in a tree house (built on stilts). All food, lodging, and safari trips were included in the package deal. For once Don didn't have to drive, but it sure was nice and warm enough in our truck when we went ourselves to the near-by Matobo Game Park. We planned another trip to Victoria Falls and Hwanke Game Park before Bakers left.

While here J Will ran the thirteen-and-a-half-mile run at How Mine. He joined about six hundred runners and came in 450th place. Men, women, and children all participate in different age categories. Many of the blacks wore no shoes. J did well; it was a tough run, especially going uphill the first half. Downhill was much easier. First prize was $750.00 (Zimbabwe dollars).

Safari tree lodge

Grace played the piano for church. Too bad she had to leave. They could use her talent here. The regular pianist, Barry Johnson, decided to join the new church that was just started. Actually, the African people do well singing a cappella.

11
SPIRITUAL GROWTH

DON WAS ONE of the elders, and Janet enjoyed working with the teens.

We were in one of the forty SDA Churches in Bulawayo, Zimbabwe. The Bulawayo City Church is one of the few English-speaking churches in Zimbabwe. Ndebele and Shona are the two main languages here, although English is the official language.

The country of Zimbabwe has a Seventh-day Adventist membership of 11,000. There are 650 who attend where we went to church. Because of the large number of people, they have two church services each Sabbath and use the annex for the overflow of people. The Western Zambezi Conference is located next door to our church. They let us use one of the rooms upstairs for our teen Sabbath School. (I called it the Upper Room.) The youth came in their school uniforms, and they really looked sharp.

The teens went to Umguza Park one Sabbath afternoon. To begin the day we had Sabbath School followed by lunch. We had a very nice time on a walking game safari. Of course, there were no lions or other wild animals in the park. When we went a few weeks prior, we didn't see a thing. This time, with a guide, we see a giraffe, zebra, and a few antelope-type animals. Guguleightu and I were walking down the road, and we heard this thunderous noise! A little way ahead of us we saw six giraffes whiz past us. Our walk was quite long, so we didn't go on the Bible scavenger hunt. But the teens all agreed they wanted to come back again.

Giraffes we encountered on our walk

COMMUNION

On communion Sabbaths, the church is packed. More people come on this special Sabbath than any other time. One Sabbath we ran out of grape juice and had to fill more glasses before we could continue the service. This happened at both the eight o'clock and eleven o'clock services. (When there is no grape juice available in some African countries, they make raisin juice.) The lady who washed my feet did an exceptionally good job. The African people are very devoted to God and church. They are very spiritually minded and love God.

Solusi students and pastors came to our church that same Sabbath. They were trying to raise money the government was requiring them to raise so that they can become a university. The money is surety that the school will keep running. Of course, Solusi has been operating for over 100 years, so I suppose it is just another gimmick.

HILLSIDE DAM CHURCH POTLUCK

Be sure to bring your own plate, silverware, and cup if you expect to eat.
   Sabbaths our church has a monthly potluck at Hillside Dam. It is a beautiful warm day today. We brought Titsi, our domestic worker, for her first time. She is enjoying the food and is becoming acquainted with other young people.

OUR CHURCH PASTOR

Pastor Eddie Lea was our pastor in Bulawayo. He was the last of the Caucasian pastors in Zimbabwe. He and his and his wife, Margaret, will be moving to South Africa soon.

Pastor Lea was telling our Sabbath school class about the soup line in Bulawayo. The Catholics started it in 1986. They feed the street people around the railroad station. People just go there after dark and sleep on the street.

Different churches conduct a soup kitchen for these street people. The Seventh-day Adventist Church is scheduled for Thursday nights. They hire a lady to make the soup and then a pastor or elder takes it and volunteers to serve the soup in tin cans. About 100 street people appreciate and enjoy a hot meal.

Following Pastor Lea, Pastor Marchemery became our next pastor who stayed until he left for America to study health ministries. His plan was to return to his home church and relate to them the advantages of healthful living. However, he never came back.

PRAYER MEETINGS

We conducted prayer meetings in church members' homes on Wednesday nights. The members of our Sabbath School class took turns going to each other's home. This is a good way to get acquainted as well as receive a spiritual blessing.

EVANGELISTIC CRUSADE

Calvin Rock conducted an evangelistic crusade in Bulawayo Centennial Park. There were about 500 baptized after that crusade. After the first week, there was a baptism for SDA former members and children of SDA parents. About 160 were baptized. A very good result. One Friday night Pastor Rock went over the doctrines of the church thoroughly.

We met Walter Veith and his wife at a church retreat south of Matobo by a little lake. He was our guest speaker who spoke on evolution and health, which included a vegan diet.

CAMP MEETING AT GWERU

Gweru, a town about 100 miles from Bulawayo, is a two-hour drive. We enjoyed the Sabbath worshiping with others of like faith. Gweru has two campmeetings. One for whites and one for coloreds. The Zambezi Conference has five churches that are mixed white and colored. There is also a black campmeeting for the SDA Field Churches.

VISIT FROM GC PRESIDENT FOLKENBURG

Elder Folkenburg, the then-new president of our General Conference, was here for a special event. He was accompanied by the outgoing GC president, Neal Wilson, who helped him become acquainted with our country. There were so many people we had to have the meetings outdoors. People brought blankets and sat on the ground. Ladies brought umbrellas to keep the sun off. The sun shines very brightly in Bulawayo. The large choir was outstanding.

12
"IT'S ABOUT TIME"

THE YOUNG PEOPLE in all forty Seventh-day Adventist churches in and around Bulawayo are beginning a three-week "Youth Evangelistic Crusade" downtown at the outdoor amphitheater. They have chosen speakers from each church, and a big turnout is expected with God's help. This involves special prayers and lots of hard work of organizing on the part of the young people and youth department pastors from the Zambezi Union and Western Union Conference. Winning many people to Jesus Christ is their goal.

Many non-church members are attending. The youth crusade is geared toward young people, so I decided to go. I was the only white person I saw and the oldest. Ha! Actually, I took Titsi, our domestic worker.

Two weeks later

The Youth Crusade is three-fourths over. Six pastors, at the same time, baptized 276 youth Sabbath afternoon in the BASS (Bulawayo Adventist Secondary School) swimming pool. Another baptism is scheduled for next Sabbath afternoon, the last day of the crusade.

ONE WEEK LATER

This second Sabbath 132 more are being baptized. Many are young people from different SDA schools. Evidently, our SDA schools don't conduct baptismal classes for their students, so it is beneficial for them to have these meetings

Together over 400 were baptized on two Sabbaths in the BASS (Bulawayo Adventist Secondary School) swimming pool. This took place during one of the cool winter months, July, here in Zimbabwe. It was about 10 degrees Celsius (50 F). Titsi Mussezehi, our domestic worker, was among those who were baptized on this very cold winter day. Twenty-one years old is a wonderful time to give your heart to Jesus. Candidates wore their regular street clothes, and some didn't have towels to dry. Titsi appreciated the warm coat I happened to have in our car.

They do things differently here. Titsi was very happy that she was baptized into the Seventh-day Adventist Church. She will join a baptismal class on Sabbaths, because I'm sure there are a lot of things she is not familiar with in the Bible. When a call is made, and people accept, you can't very well turn them down. I talked to one of the pastors in charge, and he said as long as she doesn't smoke, drink, believe in ancestral worship, and knows about the Sabbath, they will baptize her. It was very cold in that swimming pool. Titsi said she would have been baptized even if she knew it was so cold. Someone sent Bibles in our first shipment, so Titsi chose one she liked.

Titsi and Janet

Titsi was baptized

YOUTH MARCH ON BULAWAYO

The mayor of the city along with Ron Forde, another one of the dentists at ADP, and I were asked to be judges at the "Prevention of AIDS AND ALCOHOL Contest." We were announced as two of the dentists from the Adventist Dental Clinic, and if they needed any work done on their teeth, they should go to our dental clinic. That was a nice plug for us. We voted on who gave the best speech, had the best content, and best presentation. It wasn't easy to choose, as everyone participating presented interesting and informative facts against AIDS and Alcohol, and the prevention as well as the results and risks of AIDS and Alcohol. All the Adventist churches were represented in the contest and there was a very good turnout of people who enjoyed the presentation.

EASTER

The biggest holiday in Zimbabwe is Easter. It is a four-day Easter Holiday. Good Friday, Holy Sabbath, Easter Sunday, and Easter Monday. Easter seems almost as big as Christmas here. Stores close, people are off work, and there is no school Friday through Monday.

Easter Sunday morning we went to Russells' to view the heavens through their telescope. Mars, Mercury, Saturn, and Jupiter were all visible. We could see four Jupiter moons, and we saw the rings around Saturn. We also got to view the Southern Cross. It is similar to the northern hemisphere's Big Dipper and the North Star.

WOMEN'S MINISTRIES

I attended a Women's Ministries retreat at Shalom camping area. How peaceful it was. The deep spiritual life and commitment to God is especially impressive as we studied about prayer with Richard O'Ffill's CDs. We were drawn closer to Jesus associating with our African friends.

OUTREACH

St. George handicapped children really enjoyed a picnic lunch and a fun day at Malami Dam in Matobo National Park. The gnats were dreadful, but only bothered the spectators who were sitting around watching the children's activities. Mavingires, Munzeywas, and Mlalazies were the families who so willingly made this a wonderful day for the St. George handicapped children.

13
FURLOUGH HOME

EVERY TWO YEARS for two months in Zimbabwe's winter we boarded a plane and headed for home. There is an eight-hour time difference from Zimbabwe to America.

First stop was in Washington, D.C., where we visited Jan and Verland Ernston. It had been a while since we had seen them in Zimbabwe. They showed us around the sights in Washington, D.C. Lincoln Memorial, Washington Monument, and the White House are travelers' favorite places to see. The Library of Congress where they have a large replica of the White House is very impressive. And we visited the General Conference Headquarters of our church, also. The cherry blossoms were a sight to see.

It was wonderful seeing our families again. They listened attentively while we told of our experiences in Africa. Some even planned to make that trip to Zimbabwe to enjoy the time of their life.

After making our rounds to visit family and friends, we headed for Fredericksburg, Texas, to make sure Janet's mother was ready to go back to Zimbabwe with us. She was packed, had gotten her vaccinations, passport, and round-trip ticket and was ready to make the trip to an unfamiliar foreign country with us.

Our seventeen-hour lay-over time in Amsterdam while waiting for our plane to take us to Harare, Zimbabwe, was quite an ordeal. It was bitterly cold. Not having adequate clothing for the very cold weather, we nearly froze. However, we were determined to see those Holland tulips we'd dreamed of seeing. So we visited the flower market and a cheese factory also. Arriving back in Africa was a good feeling.

Mother found out she loved Africa. After staying the three months allowed, we renewed her passport for another month. That was the limit for visitors to stay in Zimbabwe.

14
GRASSHOPPERS, SLUGS, SNAILS, AND CHONGOLOLOS

As any teacher knows, there is more to teaching than reading, writing, and math.

The kindergarten children were very co-operative while taking their school readiness test. Did you know being able to tie your shoes and walking backward were part of this test?

Geneva administered the seventh- and eighth-grade pre-entry student exams. Subjects were English and math. Next year will be the exam for Ndebele. Their grade determines where they will be accepted at secondary school (high school) the following year.

At the Zimbabwe Field Bible Conference, Mrs. Mlingo, Ms. Msipa, and I were asked to present material to field schools about the Bible books we use at Fairview. Most remote areas of Zimbabwe have an enrollment of 300–500 students in each school and are not self-supporting. They receive funds from our General Conference or local unions.

We got word that the Educational Directors from the East Africa Division and the Zambezi Union are coming to visit our school this coming week. That's encouraging. I'm sure the children will be on their best behavior.

14. GRASSHOPPERS, SLUGS, SNAILS, AND CHONGOLOLOS

NEW SCHOOL BUS

Our school is raising money for a new school bus. Children were grateful for those who sponsored them on their bike-a-thon. They went 50 kilometers (about 30 miles) to Matobo Hills.

Carols by Candle-light is a traditional activity that Zimbabweans enjoy each year. It's quite impressive with everyone holding a candle while lovely Christmas carols are being sung. When Fairview School put this inspiring program on they benefitted $186.00 toward our new school bus.

> *Carols by Candle-light is a traditional activity that Zimbabweans enjoy each year. It's quite impressive with everyone holding a candle while lovely Christmas carols are being sung.*

Another way the older children raised money for the bus was to take part in a spell-a-thon. I've found that African children have good memories and are good spellers.

It was a happy day when we were able to purchase our school bus. Gugu, a fifth grader, was the designer of our school bus with fancy lettering.

FAIRVIEW ADVENTIST PRIMARY SCHOOL

OUTREACH

Tomorrow we are going to distribute clothing to the street people who will be more than willing to accept what the second- and third-grade children have brought. It must be cold sleeping under a bridge in this weather. It's good this real cold weather doesn't last more than a month or two.

Queen Mary House is a place the children liked to go and take the scrapbooks they had made and sing to the ladies there.

The third and fourth graders made bookmarks to take to the old folks' home. They will sing and visit while they give their handmade gifts to the people there.

The children were anxious to present *The Allegory of Arnion*, to parents, grandparents and church members. This is a story about the controversy between Jesus and Satan,

Dorothy Forde presented *Down by The Creekbank*. This was a very special musical that everyone enjoyed. It was a lot of hard work for Dorothy and the students. Barry Johnson accompanied them on the piano.

LINDA'S LIBRARY

At school, Don helped me to set up a library for Linda's reading class.

Linda Russell appealed to several people and some churches where she got a good response of books for our school library. We take the school library books to be bound or repaired to the prison.

Through the years several ladies have helped with my reading class. Those who helped were Linda Russell, Grace Baker, and Vera Smith. Often, we announce DEAR time (drop everything and read). Mrs. Lea taught first and second grades while I was on furlough one year.

SCIENCE PROJECT

A little section was designated on the porch for our "Children's Museum of Natural Science." After studying seeds, trees, and plants, each student brought one fruit and counted the seeds. William came up with over 2,000 seeds in his paw paw. Munyaradzi got the booby prize with one orange seed (he was happy for the pencil with the story of Daniel on it).

14. GRASSHOPPERS, SLUGS, SNAILS, AND CHONGOLOLOS

There are grasshoppers, slugs, snails, and chongololos (millipedes) all in a glass case.

Our third and fourth grade science project was planting a flower garden at school. Mr. Sabanda volunteered to help the kids prepare the soil. After the children went to the nursery to pick out flowering plants, he helped them plant them. They look lovely.

It was quite crowded, and we needed to rent a room in the house next door for the Ndebele classes. With not much room we put pictures for learning the parts of speech on the ceiling. Beth did the artwork while on her visit from Texas.

Land was found for our new Fairview Adventist School. Children and parents looked forward to more room and more modern facilities. Unfortunately, we weren't there for the groundbreaking, as we would be going on permanent return back to the United States of America before the new school building is begun.

FUN TIMES

Happy 21st Birthday, Lindiwe. Surprise for my third- and fourth-grade helper.

HAT DAY—You wouldn't believe the hats the kids are coming up with!

SNAKE CRAFT DAY—made out of ties that men donated.

HAWIAN CELEBRATION DAY—Aloha, lovely leis!

FUN CRAFT DAY—what crafty displays the students came up with!

SPORTS DAY—soccer is the favorite sport with the boys. Jump rope and hopscotch please the girls.

66 CLUB—Learn the 66 books of the Bible and join the club. You will also be required to say the Ten Commandments, the twenty-third Psalm, the Beatitudes, and the Lord's Prayer. All members who complete these requirements will take a field trip to Kami Ruins. This was a real treat, and all the children fulfilled the requirements and got to go.

ICMM—I can manage myself—with Jesus' help.

Students Reverse Uniform Service Day was hilarious! Teachers wore school uniforms, while students wore whatever they chose to wear. Shila let me wear her school uniform, so with socks and oxfords, I looked the part.

SPCA—Visited the Society for Prevention of Cruelty to Animals.

Spaghetti luncheon at our house. A reward for the class who kept their desks the cleanest for a month. Good work, third grade!

Student comment after a social studies class: "At least we're not a fourth or fifth world country."

Fourth and fifth grades social studies class treasure hunt. DJ really enjoyed this one with the children.

"Good news, children! Mrs. Russell has invited our class to her home to show us Pilgrims Progress on DVD."

Field trip to Matobo Hills to climb the rock to Cecil Rhodes' grave. Why are those hundreds of lizards climbing all over the rocks? Mother, eighty-three years young, came along and climbed the mountain with the school children. I asked her if she was ready for Kenya's Mt Kilimanjaro (19,340 feet).

CHINESE DINNER

The fourth and fifth grades social studies class is excited. I asked them to bring a plate of food to our house for our Chinese dinner. We enjoyed Chinese food, Chinese games, lanterns students had made at school and Chinese cookies made by Shanie's mother who also taught the children how to make Chinese food in a wok. Kutzai's mom made delicious tofu. It was homemade as you cannot buy tofu in the stores here. We enjoyed eating together and learning about the country of China.

15
UNIQUE ENCOUNTERS WITH THE WILD

THE LEGEND GOES that the animals were very unhappy because they didn't have a safe place to live in the bush (that's the wide-open spaces in African countries). They decided to get together with man and see what could be done so they would not have to worry about their worst enemy—man—killing them. Well, the legend goes that at their meeting they decided to make safe places for the animals to live where man could only go and visit them but not to shoot them. They called these "Game Parks." Man could only visit the animals in their vehicles—like trucks and cars. They could not get out of the cars except in designated places called look-out towers. Now the animals would be safe and have their own special places to live.

HWANGE NATIONAL GAME PARK

"Wankie's" game-viewing platforms are justly famous for the opportunity they afford the visitor to view large numbers of animals at close quarters. Within the park, tour operators offer transport on game-viewing drives in open-roofed mini-buses. At most water-holes in the park, crocodiles may be seen either basking in the sun, or partly submerged in water. Their tremendous agility enables them to propel themselves up to two meters vertically above the water surface. They may lay up to seventy-five eggs on lake shores and river banks. Teeth are replaced as soon as they break or fall out; the new ones erupting from underneath the old. This may occur several times in a crocodile's life, as it has more than two sets of teeth. Crocodiles are very dangerous, and they are responsible for more human deaths than any other wild species.

> *Crocodiles are very dangerous, and they are responsible for more human deaths than any other wild species.*

We are in the Hwange Game Park with Johan Seligmann and Tristen, his four-year-old son, and Karen, the gal who came as a student missionary for a year to works at Queen Elizabeth Adventist Children's Home (QUEACH).

In our group, there are fourteen adults. After driving in the bush, we came back and compared notes on which animals we had seen. Giraffe, warthog, zebra, wildebeest, two rhinoceros, and kudu, Zimbabwe's national animal, chosen because of its great strength.

We planned to come back to camp and eat breakfast, but someone announced that they had seen a lion at the waterhole with a kill. He had been guarding it for three or four hours and also eating the young buffalo. We had to rush to see him amble off, then dash across the road and into the bush. The vultures came from all directions. The jackals and hyenas all tried to get their share. There was nothing left in the morning when we went back, only a skeleton and not much of that. However, those vultures were still there.

Saturday night we went to the Safari Lodge waterhole where we were told the animals come at night. We missed seeing forty elephants by five minutes we were told. We saw one elephant by the side of the road along with hyenas, a honey badger, waterbuck, spring rabbit, two wild dogs (rare), a very stately sable, and a whole family of baboons sitting in the middle of the road. Babies on their mother's backs, all sizes are a sight to see. We saw steenbok that are the size of a fawn and have two small horns. A very cute duiker and a bat-eared fox caught our attention.

NEXT MORNING

We got up very early this morning but haven't seen very much exciting game until now. We just came across four young male lions in the middle of the road. Don is slowing down, and I am fumbling with the camera. They are about four or five feet from our car. Karen is riding with us. One of the lions just stood up and startled Karen. She is so scared she's rolling up the window quickly. The window is closed, but the handle came off. Evidently, the lions aren't hungry, as they are not trying to attack us. It's been about a half an hour, and we are still enjoying our rare find.

POACHERS

Poachers have been a menace since Independence, 1980. Christmas day 1989 four armed poachers were shot dead. If a person is seen with a gun walking inside the game park, the guards will assume he is a poacher wanting to kill an elephant. The guard will shoot the poacher on the spot. Why an African would take a chance with his life is because an African man doesn't make much money, so he will take a chance on poaching. Elephant tusks bring more money than he could earn in a year working. The elephant tusks are sold, and carvings are made from them.

Poachers also go after rhinoceros. A rhino's horn is used in medicine in China. They think when you drink from a rhino horn you will have good health and good luck, so it is very valuable. A rhino's horn is made of keratin—a soft substance like our fingernails and toenails—and will grow back if the animal hasn't been killed.

Rhinos have very poor eyesight but an extremely good sense of smell. Before going up to the look-out tower, Don decided to take some pictures of a rhino close to the tower. If the rhinoceros had gotten a scent of him, he probably would have charged. Too close for comfort!

Huge herds of African cape buffalo are often seen in the game parks. Deceptively docile in appearance, they are, in fact, among the most dangerous of wild animals.

16
ZAMBEZI CONFERENCE

OUR CHURCH ORGANIZED three new conferences. The western, central, and northern conferences. There are no more field conferences. That is progress for Zimbabwe. The difference in a field and a conference is that the field is not independent, but is supported by our General Conference.

Zimbabwe was part of the East Africa Division of the Seventh-day Adventist Church when we were there in 1988. In 2015 Zimbabwe became part of the Southern Africa-Indian Ocean Division. Headquarters are in South Africa.

Zimbabwe has a population of eleven million people and 120,000 elephants. There are twenty-four secondary schools and sixty-nine Adventist primary schools, which are mostly sponsored by the government with mostly Adventist staff.

Zambezi Union Workers' Woes

Our church family has really been going through a sad time. About a week ago Johann Seligman, the treasurer of the Zambezi Union, had a car accident going to South Africa. He is in intensive care at a Johannesburg hospital and is still in a coma although he comes out of it sometimes and speaks a little. We have been getting all sorts of reports. As the pastor said, some are optimistic, some pessimistic, and some realistic. Merle, his wife, and three children were in Johannesburg waiting for Johann to come back from

Bulawayo. That is a blessing because they are with her parents, and she can go to the hospital often, which is most of the time. Those who talk with her on the phone say she is taking this all calmly, but her mother said she thought Merle, who has multiple sclerosis and is not as steady on her feet, was in shock and is not admitting that this has happened. Sabbath afternoon they anointed Johann. All elders and others who wanted to meet for special prayer attended. At the anointing, Johann prayed about three minutes then lapsed into a semi-conscience state. Tristan, his five-year-old son, is taking this very hard.

A Few days later – Good news

Good news. Meryl said she was going to the hospital to take Johann pajamas. He is going to be put in a "lazy chair." God is answering our payers on his behalf.

Sad news

Yesterday we got a phone call from South Africa saying Johann had died. Why would God let this happen when his family needs him so much? And we have often said the Union office could not get along without him. So why did it have to be Johann? There is no earthly answer we can come up with so we must still trust God to work everything out because it is beyond our understanding. We know Johann will be raised to life again when Jesus comes back to take him to heaven.

> There is no earthly answer we can come up with so we must still trust God to work everything out because it is beyond our understanding.

MOVE FOR THE AUDITOR

The auditor, Don Pettibone and his wife, Susan, have been told they have until the end of December to leave the country. He will still be the auditor for Zimbabwe and will be coming back any time he needs to, but the government doesn't understand. The Pettibones will move to Kenya or Malawi. That means the only American expatriates left in Bulawayo are the three dentist families, besides the preacher and his wife. Pastor and Mrs. Lee have been given a few months extension before they must leave Zimbabwe and go to South Africa.

Crusade for Christ

James went to some of the meetings where there were 3,000 in attendance. The sermons were spoken in Ndebele then translated into English, so people had the opportunity of hearing them twice. Four to five hundred people were baptized in the BASS swimming pool. Six candidates were baptized at the same time by six ministers.

Shila, Ed and Linda Russell's daughter, and Shana, Dorothe and Ron Forde's daughter, are being baptized together at the same time with the same pastor holding them both together. A beautiful occasion that two friends will always have to remember.

Pastor Machamari, the Zambezi Union Secretary, has a first grader who preached a mini-sermon at the last evangelistic meeting right before his father preached at the outdoor amphitheater.

Cushion to the rescue

It is very crowded this afternoon here in Bulawayo City Park in an outdoor amphitheater. We are at an evangelistic meeting, and we did not realize all the seats would be taken, so we will do what others are doing—sit on the cement steps. Some nice lady is offering me a cushion to sit on and a spread for Don. Some have brought umbrellas to keep the sun and heat off, and we see many lawn chairs. Tomorrow we will bring our lawn chairs, sit in the shade, and make sure we get here earlier. More people come on the weekends. The speaker is a pastor from Florida. His sermons are being translated from English to Ndebele. The health talk is informative, and the music is inspiring. There will be a baptism tomorrow in the BASS (Bulawayo Adventist Secondary School) swimming pool. There were literally hundreds who came forward for baptism. The main thing that was emphasized is accepting Jesus as their personal Savior. They are baptized when they accept the Sabbath, state of the dead, and abstain from tobacco and alcohol. Of course, all the doctrines are explained during the meetings. Bible studies are given after their baptism and they are assigned to one of the many Bulawayo churches. After a year the baptized candidates are given church membership.

QUEACH—QUEEN ELIZABETH ADVENTIST CHILDRENS HOME

Gloria Pierson, the administrator of our children's orphanage in Bulawayo, asked me to hand out the long-stemmed carnations to the kindergarten graduates after they received their diplomas. The children looked adorable in their graduation caps with red tassels and navy-blue capes. I made thirteen corsages and three boutonnieres for the occasion. It was my privilege to serve on the QUEACH board for seven years.

Karen came from Europe as a volunteer for a year working at QUEACH. Presently there are a very limited number of missionaries in our Queen Elizabeth orphanage here in Zimbabwe as the nationals are now capable of carrying on present duties.

On several occasions, Ed and Linda Russell treated groups of children from the orphanage to several places of interest around town.

The QUEACH Christmas party was held at the Bulawayo SDA City Church. What fun it was to see all those children's happy faces as they played games and opened their presents. The delicious food was gobbled up quickly. It was a happy group of children who went back to their orphanage.

17
MARVELOUS MALAWI LAKE

From Harare, we flew into Malawi, then took a bus to the Club Makokolo Hotel on Lake Malawi, where we stayed during our second PASDAD convention. We showed up late, but they still put on the traditional show where they cater to tourists. Lots of African music with drums and marimbas, and traditional dancing.

We enjoyed the boat ride that took us to the southern tip of Malawi Lake. It was good having Mother with us on this interesting, very large boat excursion. PASDAD chartered this boat for all members and their wives. Jumping off the top of the boat was refreshing for those who chose to enjoy the water.

While I attended PASDAD classes for continuing education, Janet and Mother relaxed and enjoyed the warm sun shining on the sandy beach. Malawi is truly a paradise with the most pleasing weather in all of Africa.

EMERGENCY CLINIC

Refurbished equipment came for our emergency clinic from Loma Linda School of Dentistry, provided by the Loma Linda Alumni Association. Our emergency clinic is located in back of the dental practice. Also, there is a room for the lab man who does dentures and partials. In the emergency clinic, there are some patients who are unable to pay, although most patients have the means. It is a walk-in clinic with no appointment necessary. No one is turned away. The three of us dentists rotate working in the emergency clinic every three weeks.

18
SOLUSI COLLEGE

SOLUSI IS THE first foreign mission school our church started in southern Africa in 1894. There is a secondary boarding school on the same campus. The non-boarding elementary school has about 300 primary (elementary) school students. 250 students attend college; as well as 235 students in the secondary school (high school).

"We hear so much about Solusi College it's time we go for a visit." Solusi is located thirty miles from Bulawayo. About ten of the thirty miles is dirt road. 8,000 acres is left of the 12,000 acres that Cecil Rhodes gave Solusi in the late 1800s.

Police stopped us wanting to know what we have in our truck. "Food and chairs for the church potluck," we informed them.

We saw a variety of nut trees and fruit trees, including oranges and lemons on the college campus. The college grows several vegetables, also. Most of the land is used for cattle. We bought some delicious naartjie (tangerines). Growing on the campus of Solusi are beautiful African tulip trees and poinsettia trees that are fifteen to twenty feet tall.

Today the man preaching is from America. So they are translating his sermon into the Ndebele language. For their special item (special music), a men's group is singing in Ndebele. Such a blessing to hear such inspirational music. No accompaniment is necessary.

Solusi College became a university after some improvements and is now affiliated with Andrews University in Berrien Springs, Michigan. To achieve university status, they had to pave the road to the school and move the secondary and primary schools off campus. I'm not sure about the school for the blind children. Before we left, they built a new primary school and secondary trade school. They built a women's dorm also. This year Solusi University celebrated its one-hundredth year in Christian education.

Solusi has progressed from missionary educators to being almost completely operated by Adventist national educators. Presently there are a very limited number of missionaries in our university, secondary schools, and primary schools.

> *Solusi has progressed from missionary educators to being almost completely operated by Adventist national educators.*

The very old graveyard adds interest to Solusi. This graveyard is where many of the early church workers and missionaries are buried. The sister of Pearl Barnam, a friend from Alabama, and her husband were among those who sacrificed their lives as missionaries in Zimbabwe. They were murdered in the Eastern Highlands of Zimbabwe while doing missionary work and are buried in this gravesite on the campus of Solusi.

This afternoon we are touring Solusi campus driving on some of the 8,000 acres and climbing a couple of mountains. It is nearly dark. The moon is full and bright and beautiful.

NEWSPAPER HEADLINES — NEW $90M VOCATIONAL SCHOOL

"The government's goal of providing education to every child has received a massive boost with the building of a nine million dollar ($1 million US dollars) vocational school at Solusi Mission near Figtree, Zimbabwe.

The new school will offer a wide range of academic subjects as well as agriculture, building, woodwork, fashion and fabric, food and nutrition. Most of these subjects are not being offered under the existing curriculum.

The director of ADRA (Adventist Development and Relief Agency) who is coordinating the project said Mr. Armondo Lopaz would accept the candidates who met the entry requirements regardless of religious affiliation.

The bulk of the funds, about six million dollars, were provided by the Protestant Centre for the development, ADRA. The rest of the money came from the Adventist churches in Zimbabwe. The Adventist Secondary School has 235 pupils. Enrollment will increase when the facility is complete."

19
FUN TIMES

The church social committee worked hard on planning socials for our church. I enjoyed working with them. Our Valentine's Party for gals and guys was enjoyed by all. Decorations and food were exceptional.

Our progressive dinner helped us become better acquainted. A progressive dinner is interesting as you go from one house to another enjoying the different courses of the meal.

Thanksgiving Day celebration. Fifty missionaries from all denominations living in Zimbabwe got together on Thanksgiving to celebrate an American Thanksgiving Day dinner.

Each year on the Fourth of July, we love getting together with our fellow Americans for a Fourth of July party.

Arnetts' New Year's party—ping pong, music, games, fireworks, fun, and food. Ed and Gloria Pierson picked up fireworks in South Africa to help bring in the New Year. Thirty-six came including fourteen children, who enjoyed swimming in the pool. It was interesting watching everyone trying to stay awake until midnight.

Jan and Verland Ernston treated us to a "Have it your way" dinner. How interesting to see—you may order the dessert first, the fork without the potato salad, the butter and no bread—not knowing the disguised names for each item. A very fun time for good sports.

Dorothy and Ron Forde entertained twenty people in their backyard by their swimming pool. Delicious food and lots of fun.

"**THE MAGIC OF CHRISTMAS**"—Flowers and carols presented by the association of Bulawayo floral groups. Floral arrangements were designed by several floral groups while Christmas carols were being sung by various singing groups.

African Christmas—A typical African Christmas is when the kids swim in Russells' swimming pool. The Russells' two girls, Shila and Amy; Fordes' three children, Shana, Tony, and Kim; Piersons' two boys, Kenny and Jeremy.

TV comes on half a day. The license costs $300.00 Zimbabwe dollars a year so we don't have to listen to any commercials. A lot of political programs and a few black sitcoms like *Amen* and *The Cosby Show* are the usual programs. There is local news, also.

Daughter Debbie kept us supplied with videos—some educational; some entertaining.

Zimbabwe Broadcasting Company got new background music for the news. An African was beating the drums—real neat. We got *Voice of America* on our short-wave radio, so we could hear some of the news from home.

HERE COMES THE BRIDE

African weddings are quite different. The one I witnessed started only forty minutes late. An interpreter translated in the Shona language. The groom is from Harare, where they speak Shona in that part of the country. He is a new graduate pastor. We started with church hymns and other sacred songs; then we sang more church songs, and then the bridal march. The bridal recessional is played on a keyboard. The beautiful three-tiered, heart-shaped cake, made by one of our church ladies, was placed on the platform. It was a nice ceremony but very long. It took the bride ten minutes to walk down the aisle. They do a slow little dance step while going down the aisle. And out, also. Not only the bride and her attendants but the groom and his five attendants, plus five junior attendants, a tiny bride and groom, Bible boy, and candle lighters.

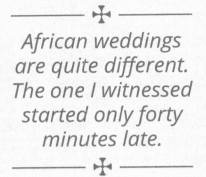

African weddings are quite different. The one I witnessed started only forty minutes late.

After the wedding, the bride, groom, and two attendants had to sign several certificates. They did it right on the platform on the table next to the cake. The minister asked all married couples to repeat their wedding vows again, and the minister's wife said a few words of advice to the bride and groom. About a dozen times during the ceremony activities, some lady made this real shrill noise with her mouth, like Indians do. This is all part of the wedding proceedings. The bridal recessional was played on the keyboard as the wedding party left for the reception, which followed in the fellowship hall.

20
VICTORIA FALLS, THE GREATEST SHOW ON EARTH

AT THE WESTERNMOST corner of Zimbabwe, the Zambezi River, the longest river in the world, suddenly tumbles three hundred and fifty feet into a series of deep gorges. The water falls so far and hits the bottom with such a force that it sprays back up to the top and on into the sky. This is Victoria Falls. The spray from the falls can be seen from forty miles away. Some days, when the clouds are low, the spray from the falls rises until it joins the clouds in the sky. On the average, 550 cubic meters of water go over the falls every minute. Victoria Falls has the largest curtain of falling water in the world and is one of the Seven Natural Wonders of the World.

Tourists hike to the edge of the falls, where they stand with nothing between them and the bottom. There is no fence or railing, and the rock at the edge is always wet and slippery.

The first European known to have seen Victoria Falls was a Scottish missionary, David Livingstone, one of the great white explorers of Africa. David Livingstone was very impressed with the falls. He wrote in his diary that the angels must have circled back in their flight just to have a second look, so awesome is it all. There is a statue of David Livingston near Victoria Falls.

Victoria Falls is named after England's Queen Victoria since England ruled Zimbabwe at that time.

We took a small airplane ride, named the "Flight of the Angels," over the falls. Taking that ride was a thrilling thing to do! The rainbow over the falls was very beautiful.

On the bridge dividing Zimbabwe and Zambia, we were surprised to see people bungee jumping. That's not our idea of having fun; these people were daring to take a chance on their lives.

21
MOTHER MUST LEAVE—RULES OF THE COUNTRY

MOTHER HAS STAYED her allotted time of three months, and like the first visit, we extended her stay for another one month. Sadly, it is time for Mother to leave and go back home to Texas. We took Mother to Les Saisons for her 86th December birthday before she left.

After driving Mother to the Harare Airport, she met Pastor Baraka Muganda, the East Africa Ministerial Secretary. We had arranged for Pastor Muganda to meet her there. He was waiting for her, to make sure she got on the planes necessary to get her home safely. She appreciated the traveling companion and help he gave her. God worked it out for Mother.

Mother loved Africa and said, "I think I left my heart in Africa."

She loved the game parks, Victoria Falls, church activities, and Africa in general. I appreciated her helping me with school work while she was here.

It was a sad day when we learned just three months after Mother got home, that she had cancer. She spent her last days with my sister and passed away on Easter Sunday. We were able to go to her memorial service. The only drawback of being a missionary is leaving family and not being there for important occasions, like children's birthdays, graduations, and weddings.

Mother and DJ

MAIL DELIVERY

The next best thing to being home is receiving mail from family and friends. Although it took a long time for some mail to arrive, we enjoyed the letters and cards we received.

One letter took thirty-two days.

Another letter took two and a half months to arrive.

A letter from Don's dad made a side trip to Zambia and arrived a couple of weeks late.

Beth, my daughter, and her husband, Chris, sent a letter and birthday card for my December 12th birthday. It was dated December 1, 1988. It is now July 1989, and I am just now getting to read it.

Our postage and phone rates went up about forty percent.

22
DROUGHT WOES

WE ARE EXPERIENCING the worse drought in Zimbabwe in ten years. Everyone is waiting for rain. The farmers need it badly. Sugarcane growers have no water for irrigation. The result is no sugar. Oilseed crops are a disaster leaving a shortage in cooking oil.

One of the saddest things is that the cattle have no meal, and the chickens no corn or feed, which means no eggs. Dairy farmers are selling off milk cows for meat. The water pans dried up in the bush, and many animals have died.

Zimbabwe grew plenty of corn, but the government exported it to South Africa and other countries. So, when the drought came, there wasn't enough for the Zimbabweans. The domestic workers have to stand in long queues (lines), and sometimes when they get there, they have run out of mealie meal. Then they have to go back the next day and wait again. White corn is very scarce. The United States sent yellow corn, but the Zimbabweans were not happy. They want white corn. Mugabe sold the white maize to South Africa.

Janet saw a delivery truck heading to the city, so she chased the truck carrying maize to one of the grocery stores. She waited for it to arrive and managed to buy a couple of sacks for our hired help. Otherwise, they will have to wait in those long queues to buy some.

The city of Bulawayo started watering rationing the 15th of January. Overuse led to fines. If anyone still overused, they put a restriction in the pipes to reduce water flow to a dribble. We hadn't had enough rain to keep the dam that supplies the city water more than 13 percent full. The problem was that the pipeline from the dam was too small to pump enough water to keep up with the water usage. The city cut us to 660 liters a day or about 175 gallons. This was per household, so it gives us more between the two of us and our domestic workers than a family of four or five would have.

The government is in the process of building another pipeline; at least they have made the money available. It will, in all likelihood, be about three years in getting to completion as the Chinese are doing the job. This means about three years of water rationing unless the rains come.

The city is going to cut our allotment of water even more. Down from 660 liters to 600. That is from 175 to 130 gallons per day. We still have enough water if we don't use it for watering the yard. This month we were about 300 gallons under our allotted usage, so I need to have James water some of the plants. James uses bath water to wash clothes or water the plants and the yard.

LATER

> The drought has gotten worse; they have lowered the water ration to 300 liters per day. (sixty-five gallons) The country is just dried out.

The drought has gotten worse; they have lowered the water ration to 300 liters per day. (sixty-five gallons) The country is just dried out. Trees are dying as well as the shrubs. I can't be sure how many trees are dying as it is the end of winter and some of the trees have not put on their new leaves yet.

We thought we had it made, as the reading was well within limit. Then we found out the meter was in gallons instead of liters. This means that we were over our limit of water by about double the amount allowed. So we have been really conservative this past week, and we are now almost back to normal limits. It is amazing how much water is used just flushing the toilet. As the saying goes, "If it's yellow, let it mellow; if it's brown, flush it down."

We had a little rain this past week, but not enough to help our city water supply. Last week I got a 1,000-gallon tank to store water in from the deep well at the Zambezi Union.

I have been monitoring the water for the past few weeks, and we have been well within the daily ration quota. I have enough saved up that I could put some in the pool. I am not sure how long before we will have to go on a lower amount when they cut our rations. We were on half of what we are allowed since the last drought we had. I checked our water tank, and we have about 500 gallons stored in our storage tank.

James has been helping me put a cover of black plastic over the swimming pool. We can't add water to replace what would be lost by evaporation. I guess the plastic will stay there for the duration of the drought.

Things may continue to go up in price on all staples. The humidity is so low it is almost like being in the desert. The grass, roots and all, have just disappeared from the yard. When it rains I hope we get some gentle, soft rain for several weeks. Otherwise, the topsoil will wash away.

This past week I hauled about 500 gallons of water home from the Zimbabwe Union. The water is not fit to drink, so we are in the process of putting in a pump on the holding tanks we have at each dentist's home. This way with the holding tank connected to the house we can have water when the city water is gone.

One of the side effects of the drought is the lack of water to generate electricity. The dental practice is in the process of getting a diesel generator to supply the dental office and a generator for each home.

Some of our trees died. James is trying to revive some of the fruit trees and keep the roses alive. The peach, plum, and apricot trees seem to be doing well. The citrus trees are in very poor shape. We have lost about six trees, four cedars, one lemon, and one flowering tree of local origin. We are about another month off from the rainy season. The city council is expected to lower the water allotment to 200 liters next week. That is about fifty-two US gallons per day. Still enough for us to get by without too much of a hardship.

We use the kitchen water to water the outside plants. If we don't use the water, it will not carry over to the next month. They say, "Use it or lose it."

There is a rumor that all South African countries with 20,000 people are migrating to Bulawayo from rural areas because of lack of water and food. They will become squatters with no home or source of income. The government must feed them and maintain some form of law and order or crime becomes rampant.

The shipment of corn is beginning to be delivered to Zimbabwe. So far, there has been shipped about 200,000 tons of corn from the United States. A lot of corn. We have not seen the results yet; the corn has not reached the stores. Maybe this week the millers will start supplying the stores with enough so the long queues will disappear.

The electric power is soon to be rationed by cutting the power off in different areas of the city. Our area will be turned off several times each week; only one day will it be off in the evening. We have bought a gas light to use at that time.

FUEL

The country has been running a campaign to get people to save fuel. I think I will fill up several drums with diesel just in case they decide to ration the fuel. The problem is that they don't have the money to buy the fuel and get everything else they want, so they may ration fuel. On the way home from work I filled up the fuel tank. Gasoline is up to $10.75 per gallon; diesel is $5.16 per gallon. I am sure glad we have diesel vehicles. Even with diesel, I put in a little over $100.00 in fuel. That is a lot even in Zimbabwe dollars.

So far, I have nearly filled up a drum (sixty gallons) with diesel fuel. This should act as a small buffer in case they raise the price again, or it could even become scarce.

23
BRAVE BETH

Daughter Beth flew all the way from Texas alone to visit us. We picked her up at the Harare Airport, and thus began her month encounter with the wilds of Africa.

We spent four days enjoying Wankie Game Park and Victoria Falls.

At Wankie we rounded the curb and right in the middle of the road was a beautiful leopard. Leopards are not usually seen in daylight, so that was a real treat. We saw just about every animal in the game parks we went to.

We splurged and spent two days and nights at a tree lodge camp. We had a game guide and most of the comforts of home. We saw lots of animals including an adorable baby giraffe. It must have been a newborn as it had its umbilical cord still hanging. We saw another baby and several mother giraffes, too. Two rhino we chased down the road (in the truck, of course).

While here, Beth redecorated the dental office waiting room. It wasn't long before the new curtains came for the main waiting room. It had needed to be fixed up for a long time.

Beth and I went into town and found quite a few shops to explore. Beth got some souvenirs and gifts to take back home with her. She also bought many items from the town of Kadoma to sell back home: tablecloths, doilies, handmade crafts, wood carvings, and pictures. If she doesn't sell them, she will have lots of gifts to give away.

There was a trading place by the side of the road when we went to Matobo. Beth had fun trading a few items she had brought along from the States. She traded her watch for some African décor, for one. Beth enjoyed being here, and she was surprised that we did so much. She thought she would be bored so brought along several books to read while here. Needless to say, she never had time for reading.

It was a five-hour drive to Harare to take Beth back to the airport. On the way, we stopped at the Lion and Cheetah Park where there are several lions, gemsbok, cheetah, and many caged and fenced animals. Some of these animals we have never seen before. The cheetah was in a cage, and the lions were in a place that they could not have hidden if they had wanted to.

Beth and I rode horses at the game park. We were glad the rhinos shared their reserve with us! Rhinos have a good sense of smell but not good eyesight. Our experienced guide knew exactly where to lead our horses. We rode one and a half hours on the horse trails. The guide was informative and helpful. We got real close to five rhinos. Two were a mother and baby. I didn't feel scared once I got on the horse. This is my last horse ride until the New Earth.

Beth surprised us with a painting of the elephant she saw in Africa by the waterhole. We must have disturbed him, as he came charging towards us. He stopped short for some reason, so we know God worked that out, too. This is a special painting we will always cherish.

24
LIFE IN THE VILLAGE

TAKING A RIDE out to the villages, we see an altogether different African lifestyle. Ladies are sweeping their dirt yards beside their mud huts which are made with sticks, twigs, or thatch. Some have tin roofs or thatch roofs. Whatever material is available around the village is what they use. Outside they are cooking on wood fires. The women are coming back from the river after washing their clothes and dishes and children in the water. Children, parents, and grandparents usually live with aunts and uncles in the same village. They call this the extended family.

Fishing is something many Zimbabweans love. They make fishing nets from vines or spear fish with sticks that are cut from trees and sharpened on rocks. They sometimes make boats with light balsa wood that floats. While the men hunt and fish, the women tend the gardens and grind corn into flour. Young boys tend cows. Babies go everywhere strapped to their mothers' backs. Young girls help their mothers and at the same time watch over the babies. In the village everybody helps; everybody works.

> *The people are also very family oriented. They will work and help a sibling through school rather than pursue a career for themselves.*

The people are also very family oriented. They will work and help a sibling through school rather than pursue a career for themselves. Their first obligation is to their family. They do not have many nursing homes because families take the older members to live with them.

Sadza made from maize (corn) is the staple food of Zimbabweans whether they live in the village or in town. It is cooked and stirred with a long paddle made from a stick until very stiff, and then they put meat, vegetables, or lacto (like sour milk) on the sadza. Mealies is eaten at most every meal, made either as a corn flour pudding or bread. The women grind the corn between two rocks. They might have melon, mangoes, or wild berries with their meal. On special occasions one of the village goats will be roasted. Tea is served in gourds. A sweet potato biscuit (cookie) is for dessert.

The boys play ball in the streets. Their ball looks very different. It's made from strips of cloth and a multitude of rubber bands. It seems to work quite well. The children are very happy.

25
SEEING THE REAL AFRICA

WHAT AN EXPERIENCE we had seeing how the majority of Africans live.

Friends of ours, Verland and Jan Erntson, and we started out on our African thirty-day vacation trip. We were both driving in our four-wheel drive vehicles fitted with extra fuel tanks, to make sure we could make the trip between service stations. We traveled close to 10,000 kilometers. Verland is the treasurer of the Zambezi Union, and Jan is secretary to the union president.

The first day we left early and drove to the Zambia border and then on to Riverside Farms, one of our Seventh-day Adventist supporting organizations sponsored by Wildwood Wellness Center in Wildwood, Georgia. This is where they teach agriculture and nutrition to the local people. We spent the night there in their guest house and were treated very well. The next day we got up early and drove 200 kilometers to Mbeya, Tanzania. On the way, we were stopped by several policemen at road checks for inspection of our vehicles and their contents plus our travel documents.

We had reservations and thought we had arrived at the right hotel. What a surprise when we got up the next morning when in daylight we realized the hotel we had reservations for was right next door.

The next day we drove about 650 kilometers to Morogoro, Tanzania. We thought the roads were bad in Zambia until we arrived in Tanzania. It was a challenge for Don and Verland to drive while trying to avoid hitting all the potholes. My head hit the car ceiling only once. But the country was beautiful, green, and mountainous. There were toll stations every 200 or so kilometers. We had to pay the toll in US dollars, which was $3.00 per station.

The fourth day we drove to Arusha and passed very near to Mount Kilimanjaro, the tallest mountain in Africa. We didn't have time to climb up the 19,341-foot mountain this trip. We spent Friday night and Sabbath at the Seventh-day Adventist Union headquarters. Sunday we were taken by the treasurer, George Wheeler, to several different Maasai villages. These are a group or tribe of Africans that have resisted any change, and they mainly herd cattle. They don't like having their picture taken unless you pay them. They allowed us to video their ceremony, which was a junior elder becoming a senior elder of their tribe when he became forty years old. The wife has the privilege, if she was a virgin at her marriage, of shaving her husband's head with a razorblade after the mother-in-law shaves the first few strokes. The other Maasai members form a circle around the ceremony while dancing and chanting. Most of the Maasai wore their traditional clothing, but when we looked down at their feet, we had to smile when we noticed they had on tennis shoes. Zimbabwe won first place in the commercial contest seen on TV advertising BATA shoes. The people realize that shoes make life easier.

At the last village, there was much singing and dancing. Women in a circle start the rhythm going while the men have their own activities. We figured out the idea is to keep in step with body movements which is more like jumping, with the lady opposite you. Jan and I found out it takes some concentration, but we finally caught on as they started to clap. Then they invited us to eat with them. We tried hard to be polite, and we were grateful for their hospitality. We were with them most of the day all because they knew George Wheeler, their friend whom they liked. He is a true missionary. He doesn't refuse their food no matter how horrible it tastes, and he has learned their language so he can relate to them. Of course, we couldn't take pictures until the headman said it was OK, and we had taken his picture first. They also allowed us to visit one of their huts. On the way back, the Lutheran minister, a former Maasai who accompanied us, invited us to his house for a meal. They served us boiled eggs, some very

25. SEEING THE REAL AFRICA

sweet tea, and a cup of sour milk with hominy and meal. It would take us a while before we could ever become accustomed to their diet.

We left Arusha and headed for the Ngorongoro Crater, home of 30,000 animals. The Flycatcher Inn was a farmhouse converted into a lodge. It was located just outside the park, but we had to drive way out into the bush on narrow dirt roads to find it. We passed fields and fields of wheat. Since it was so far out we were about the only guests, but they treated us like royalty, and the food was delicious.

Traveling on, we came to the Black Rhino Inn where we stayed while viewing the Ngorongoro Crater. It was the very opposite of the Flycatcher Inn. Everything was so humid the sheets were wet. No private bathrooms so we had to use the community bathroom. A very unpleasant experience, but we will say this for them, they did wash our vehicles.

We hired a guide to go with us into the Ngorongoro Crater since the guides know just where the different kinds of animals are. We spent most of the day enjoying God's beautiful creatures. It was such a treat to see stately lions, several hippopotamus, hyenas, wildebeest, hartebeest, Cape buffalo, numerous gazelles, entertaining monkeys, lovely ostrich, and hundreds of gorgeous flamingos.

After the crater, we headed for the Serengeti Plains, another huge game park in the western part of Tanzania. Along the way, we saw all sorts of animals and ostriches. The lodge we stayed in was nice and new, but no hot water to take a bath. There were rock hyrax that came and ate whatever food anyone would give them. Early the next morning we heard a low growl but didn't venture out to see what it was. As we left the hotel, we saw a large lion and took his picture. We traveled most of the day and finally crossed into Kenya. Since we had not made arrangements to stay anywhere for the night, we took a chance and stopped at one of our schools in Kenya. This is a Seventh-day Adventist institution since 1912. It was called Kamagambo Primary and Secondary School and Teacher's College. Sure enough, we were welcomed, and the president (principal, we call them in the States) took us into his home and fed us. We surely had a good sleep that night.

The next day we stopped at the University of East Africa in Eldoret, Kenya, which was one of our newer institutions. When we were leaving, someone asked us if we had room for one more to ride to the main road. Then they changed it to two. When we looked in the back seat, there were four among our belongings. When they got out, three more were waiting for a ride to the next town. The main means for transportation is walking or riding the bus.

After we left the University of East Africa, we were on our way to Mt. Elgon. This is a mountain game park that sits on the Kenya-Uganda border. We spent three enjoyable days there. Our rooms were small but nice, and we did have hot water. The lodge we stayed in was about halfway up the mountain. (7,300 feet elevation). No mosquitoes, cool nights and pleasant days. While on Mt. Elgon we made a side trip to the Saiwa Swamp, about twenty miles from our lodge. We spent most of the day there and saw some very unusual birds and animals. The deer-like animal called a sitatunga cannot be found anywhere else in the world.

We also spent three days at the Kenya Samburu National Park. The back roads to get to the lodge were mostly gravel, and the last twenty kilometers were through an area that was very bad traveling. The valley was full of lava. We were wondering what the lodge would look like since the roads were so bad. But to our surprise, it was one of the nicest places we stayed. It was new and very plush and even had a fancy mosquito net curtain all around our beds. This is where the restaurant puts bait out for the crocodiles so the guests can observe them. We rested up for our long trip to Nairobi.

It was a long drive, but we arrived at the Eastern Africa Union Adventist guest house ready for our adventures in Nairobi. We did a little shopping at the huge market, saw our medical and dental clinic and our Adventist Development and Relief Agency (ADRA) facilities, and were surprised at how crazy the people drive in that big city. We were disappointed in Nairobi thinking it was a nice, clean city. I guess Bulawayo has spoiled us. But it was interesting to see the wood carvings, pictures made from banana leaves, and many other handmade crafts.

25. SEEING THE REAL AFRICA

Our Toyota truck did a great job on our journey. One squeak caught our attention which was connected to the drive shaft. When we got to Nairobi, we managed to get a new central drive shaft bearing. That solved the problem of the squeak.

In Nairobi, we went to visit Maxwell Seventh-day Adventist Academy and saw three boys we knew from Bulawayo. Dr. Pierson's two sons, Jeremy and Kenny, and another missionary's son, Mark Pettibone. We also visited with some friends we had met at mission institute in Michigan.

After we left Mt. Elgon we started for Lake Baringo, which is located in the Rift Valley. A "luxury tent camp" was our next destination. When we arrived late in the afternoon, we were told we were not booked in the camp, but we could spend one night there. It was nice with tents, lights, bathrooms, showers, and hot water. The next day they must have felt sorry for us, as they told us we could stay on another island close by that belonged to the owner. So by boat, we arrived at our own private island. The owners were away, so it was just the four of us plus four domestic workers who took care of us making supper and breakfast the next morning. We had a nice open-air upstairs room where we woke up to the birds singing and the beautiful sunrise. They told us it was safe to swim in the lake, so Janet was looking forward to that. However, with the binoculars, I spotted a crocodile swimming in the same area. Needless to say, Janet did not swim in the lake. More people are killed by crocodiles than any other way in Africa. This is one place we hated to leave; it was so beautiful, and we saw owls in the trees looking at us with their big eyes, not usually seen in the daytime.

On our way to the largest game park in Africa, Tsavo National Park, we saw lots of animals and saw a leopard for the first time. The lodge put out bait in the tree close by to bring them close enough so we could watch them while we enjoyed our outdoor evening meal. The next day we went to Mombasa and stayed in a hotel on the beach off the Indian Ocean. Looking forward to a sight-seeing ride in a glass-bottomed boat, it turned out to be a two-foot square of glass in the bottom of the boat. The boatman took us out to the reef where we found a few pieces of coral and some shells. Friday, we hired a taxi to take us to town so we could see some of the sights and do a little shopping. One of the places we visited was the Carver's Village, a place where 3,000 African men were doing wood carvings. We purchased a few ebony pieces and some other wood carvings.

Sunday morning it was time to head home. We had to take a ferry to get on the right road. At the border, we had a little scare. Janet's passport had not been stamped right, and they didn't want to let her pass back into Tanzania. After a few minutes, we convinced them that it was just a minor error, and they allowed her to continue on the trip. We traveled through Tanzania to the Malawi border.

> *At the border, we had a little scare. Janet's passport had not been stamped right, and they didn't want to let her pass back into Tanzania.*

By the side of the road, we bought lots of baskets, of which one was a winnowing basket. Winnowing is an agricultural method for separating grain from chaff, also used to remove weevils or other pests from stored grain. Threshing, the separation of grain or seeds from husks and straw, is the step in the chaff-removal process that comes before winnowing. In its simplest form, it involves throwing the mixture into the air so the wind blows away the lighter chaff while the harvest grain falls back down for recovery. Techniques include using winnowing fans or using a tool, a winnowing fork or shovel, on a pile of harvested grain.

The crossing went smoothly, but a few kilometers down the road we were stopped for a police check. They wanted to see everything we had including reading material. We offered them some magazines, which we had brought along for such occasions. We also brought along soap, canned beef, and candy for the children.

The authorities informed us that the ladies would put on dresses before we could continue on into Malawi. The roads were being worked on and were very dusty, and by the time we neared our destination, night had

25. SEEING THE REAL AFRICA

fallen. We were glad to find a student going to our mission who directed us there. We didn't know at the time that he was taking us by the back roads, and it was ten kilometers of logging trail. We thought we would never get there. Finally, we rounded a corner and saw a light way in the distance. Upon arriving, we were surprised to find that the family was from Texas. Mrs. Pipkin was daughter Debbie's fifth-grade teacher in Keene, Texas. We had a nice visit, good food, and a restful night's sleep.

The next day we continued on our way. There was a better way out with better roads. Don and Verland were glad to drive up to 120 kilometers an hour.

We made Lilongwe around noon, ate, visited our Seventh-day Adventist dental and optical clinic, and then checked on our visas for Mozambique. After a tour of our mission in Blantyre, Malawi we spent the night in their guest house. Our Malamulo Hospital and Publishing House near Blantyre has the best hospital facilities in all of Malawi. In the hospital it is a custom for the family of the sick to come and stay all night with the patient, sleeping on the floor. Since 1902 Malamulo Hospital has been providing healthcare to one of the poorest districts in Malawi, Africa.

We joined the military convoy at the Mozambique border and picked up a European hitch-hiker who was on his way through Africa. He rode with us until we reached the Zimbabwe border. At that point, the authorities would not let him into the country because he didn't have a round-trip ticket to his home. And Mozambique would not allow him to return through Mozambique, because he had only a one-way visa. He was in trouble, but there was nothing we could do to help. The convoy had about fifty trucks and eight smaller vehicles. The Zimbabwe army led the way in their armored trucks, and we followed.

We went halfway into Tete and waited for the convoy to form for the final part of the trip. I tried to communicate with some school children while waiting, but I don't know Portuguese and not many know English. So I showed them pictures in an American schoolbook I happened to have along. With happy smiles, they just stared and pointed at the books. The quality of books, pencils, and paper is very poor. They all use exercise books covered with brown paper; one for each subject. They don't have workbooks that they can write in. School supplies are not plentiful and are expensive. Teaching in Zimbabwe, we are able to go down to South Africa and buy anything we need. Also, we brought many school supplies back with us when we returned from our furloughs.

We loved seeing the beautiful children, but we hated waiting for the convoy. However, since they are having a civil war there, we played it safe. When we reached the border, it took at least two hours to clear customs. Then we started for Harare, the capital of Zimbabwe. By the time we reached Harare, it was late, but we decided to continue on the four-and-a-half-hour drive to Bulawayo. We arrived home about two a.m.

It was so nice to be home after our very eventful, interesting, once-in-a-life-time excursion. We will always have memories of baobab trees, thatched-roof huts of clay, sticks, and grass, happy children who love getting a piece of candy, and colorfully dressed Tanzania women. Buying baskets in Kenya and Tanzania, exchanging currency in each country, baboons in the trees, potholes, animals in the wild, our Seventh-day Adventist work in so many places, police checks, crossing borders, seventy-nine exotic birds Ernstons identified, coffee and tea plantations, wheat, maize, and cotton fields, bananas everywhere, toll roads, sprite, hawkers selling their self-made crafts, friendly African people, and how good God was to us for His presence with us and a safe enjoyable journey. God definitely worked it out for all of us.

26
CHOBE NATIONAL GAME PARK

WE ARE READY with Verland and Jan for a new adventure in Chobe National Game Park in Botswana, Africa. Straight ahead we see two herds of elephants—all sizes. They are blocking the road, and we are waiting patiently for them to pass. Verland is driving, and he is not happy, because at any time those elephants could turn towards us. One of them could turn our truck over without any trouble. Well, thankfully, we see God is protecting us in this situation. The larger elephants protect their baby calves by standing all around them.

What an extraordinary appendage is the elephant's trunk! Elephants eat with them, bathe with them, sniff with them, and threaten with them. An elephant's trunk can do almost anything that a hand can do, and a whole lot more besides. Spraying water or dust bathing is among the things they do. An elephant will die of starvation if his trunk is seriously injured.

A mud bath is an elephant's idea of bliss. For as well as depositing a cooling layer on its skin, the crust formed when it dries prevents insects from biting. It also serves to deepen the waterhole itself, for over the years many tons of mud are removed. Thus, the elephants' mud baths benefit all the animals that depend on the waterhole, and provide a fascinating spectacle for the visitors.

On the street in town, we saw a donkey pulling a cart. We saw monkeys, baboon, cattle, and sheep throughout the town.

The monkey got our fruit from the car when I left the door open to go back to get something in the rondoval where we stayed overnight.

We had to watch the monkeys, as they love getting into the garbage cans.

What a variety of wonderful creatures, of all sizes, God has made for us to enjoy. Lions, giraffe, crocodile, some waterbuck, impala, lots of baboons, monkeys, and gemsbok. The Monitor lizard is about the size of a small crocodile and flips his tail like the croc.

SINAMATELLA GAME PARK

We found this special game park that is a little different than most. It isn't always easy to get reservations here, but God worked it out so we could spend three days enjoying nature and animals.

The vegetation is high and thick, and it is hard to see twenty to thirty yards from the road. The camp is situated on a mountain overlooking a narrow plain below. Our cabin is only a few feet away from the edge of the mountain, and we have an excellent view. With binoculars even the small impalas are visible. Most of the time we see elephants below eating and bathing in the mud holes. The trip here was unusual and nice with more driving than usual, but we didn't see quite as many animals as we usually do. We stayed in a thatched-roof chalet. It was six-sided with a pointed roof. Attractive.

MATOBO OUTING

Sabbath, we packed a lunch and drove to Matobo. It is such a restful place to visit. Not many people and normally a lot of wild animals. We did not see a lot of animals, but we did see a wide variety. The day was mostly overcast. It was as if the animals just stayed in bed. It was nice riding around in the quiet atmosphere. About the only sounds we could hear were the birds singing their praises to God. We saw some unusual birds, including the spoonbill and fish eagle. Saw seven crocodiles, two giraffes, three rhino, eight zebra including a baby, a rock hyrax, three hippos, two waterbuck, three klipspringers, and several impala. Oh, and of course, we saw some baboons swinging in the trees. Zimbabwe has the largest baobab trees in the world. There are 100 different kinds of cactus, small and huge in Matobo.

MATOBO HILLS

Matobo Hills lie in a National Park about forty kilometers south of Bulawayo. The Matobo refers to twelve hundred square miles of wind-sculptured granite columns, cliffs, and boulders that were formed during the flood. Great chunks of rock of different shapes and colors are stacked atop each other. Mother and Child Balancing Rocks is a famous rock formation, which consists of castle kopjes and whalebacks and resembles a mother with a child.

Africans believe their spirits still live in Matobo Hills. Within this area, which is sacred to the Matabele tribal tradition, there are also many fine ancient rock paintings. On sheltered rock faces and within the many caves to be found here, vivid scenes of hunting and animals have been left by a people now lost in the historical past. Matobo is the home of Cecil John Rhodes.

GREAT ZIMBABWE RUINS

Great Zimbabwe Ruins is composed entirely of granite blocks cut to a specific size and fitted together ingeniously without mortar. Close to a million blocks were used. It is believed building began between AD 1100 and 1150. Most was built during the fourteenth century. About 30,000 people lived there. Abandonment of Great Zimbabwe Ruins probably took place because, with so many people, water, grazing, and firewood became scarce. Drought and a plague of locusts were also a big problem. Quarrels among themselves and outside attacks on what had been a strong and united kingdom ultimately spelled its doom. President Ndlovu asked us to take the president of the Tanzania Union to the Great Zimbabwe Ruins with his wife when they were here on a visit. We had not yet been there so we enjoyed our day also.

Great Zimbabwe Ruins is a walled city with clusters of buildings, some in ruins and some standing that was very well planned and well-built. A highly organized and highly capable civilization once lived here. Of course, they have paths to follow, a museum of artifacts that have been found at the site, and a curio shop.

You can always find articles being sold by the side of the road just about any place you go. They make a lot of figurines out of soapstone. Crocheted tablecloths are popular. Some baskets and other African things usually catch our attention. They do nice crafts and work hard, so you have to give them credit for not just sitting around and doing nothing.

On Sabbath we decided to go to Matobo Game Park, about thirty miles from home. We did not expect to see many animals, but we were pleasantly surprised. We saw about nine different types of animals. We were surprised to see that the park officials had cut the horns off the rhino. They say it was done to keep the poachers from killing them for their horns. The horns are worth much money. In four years I have not heard of any poaching in Matobo Park. The park is not near any border, so we don't have poaching in this park. I wonder if they are using the horns to sell for the government. The rhino sure looks strange without horns.

At Matobo, we saw several rhinos among other animals.

LABOLA

This weekend we went with Russells to a nice place by a small lake. It was really neat. Way out where it was quiet and peaceful. We enjoyed the canoe ride, hiked up the Lebonka Resort kopjie, and found a resurrection plant with the help of a guide. The plant looks dead, but you can break off a piece, put it in water, and it comes alive.

27

HURRAY! SECOND FURLOUGH

HOME AGAIN

Our flight was sixteen hours from Johannesburg to New York with one stop in Cape Verde. Other times we went from Harare, Zimbabwe to either Germany, Amsterdam, England, or France. Our flight was always exciting and adventuresome. One layover in London we spent twelve hours sight-seeing, as we took a bus tour through the city and saw many buildings and places we had only heard about.

What a blessing to return for visits with our parents, children, grandchildren, siblings, and other members of our families and friends. Texas, Georgia, New York, and Alabama were our destinations. We were welcomed home with open arms and treated royally. Such fun we had and how the grandchildren had grown!

Karen and Todd took us to a laser show at Stone Mountain in Georgia. Dad always grew a fantastic vegetable garden that he shared with church family and neighbors. Mother Arnett was busy quilting comforters, doing ceramics, knitting, or crocheting.

The fish were biting well at Chris and Beth's lakeside home. Fishing is one of Don's favorite pastimes. We were amazed to see how expertly Alicia and her jump rope team performed, winning the state championship. Went to the Fredericksburg parade with Mother, and to the Nimitz

Museum for a little history. Johnny and Debbie drove us to Arkansas and Missouri where we enjoyed spelunking in the Ozarks and explored the Crater of Diamonds State Park as well as the Great Passion Play in Hot Springs. It was a great trip for us with Beth, Chris, Debbie, Johnny, and Alicia.

Linda and Vince took us by train from Long Island, where they live, to New York City. We saw the Statue of Liberty and visited Ellis Island. We appreciated Shirley and Ross coming from Oregon; Gilbert and Connie came up from Fredericksburg, and we managed a game of softball with the whole gang. Johnny and Debbie treated us to bed and breakfast at Crystal's Castle and a boat ride on the Bayou Queen River. Linda rode in the Hampton Classic Horse Show. She, Vince, Jared, and Alex took us on a cruise on Moriches Bay. The day ended with viewing hundreds of fireworks over New York City.

After boarding the plane and arriving in Zimbabwe, we found that Titsi had left to go and live with her mother. That meant we had to start looking for another housekeeper.

Happy is a church member and loves to sing. She has three children and husband, Joel. She would sing while my mother played our piano. Happy is very fond of my mother; they get along very well together.

When I first interviewed Happy, I couldn't understand why she would not look at me while I was talking to her. Then it was explained to me that direct eye contact during conversations is viewed as rude, especially in rural areas. Happy Malalaze is our last domestic worker.

> *When I first interviewed Happy, I couldn't understand why she would not look at me while I was talking to her. Then it was explained to me that direct eye contact during conversations is viewed as rude, especially in rural areas.*

James tries to discourage any woman who comes to work as he likes doing inside as well as outside duties. He tells them he should be doing inside; he is not a gardener. At least Happy laughs him off. They are related some way through his first wife.

DOMESTIC PROBLEMS

When we came back from furlough, we heard that James was in Ingutsheni, a local mental institution. He was picked up by the police for threatening people in town with an axe. When the doctor at the institution prescribed James lithium, he acted normal.

Unfortunately, we had to dismiss him from work. Before James left he dug up stuff we had asked him to get rid of through the years. He buried it in our backyard while being our gardener. His truck was loaded with unimaginable items as he pulled out of our yard. He had been a faithful gardener, and we will miss him.

ELFORD

We had to dismiss our next gardener, Elford, because he told so many lies, and he owed money to so many people. He had also tried to break into the other domestic quarters and got caught in the act.

One day I gave Elford orders not to use the lawn mower until I had given him instructions on how to use it. I came home and noticed how nicely the front yard had been mowed. Upon questioning him, he denied using the lawn mower and said, "Oh, no Masta, I used the scissors to cut the lawn."

The last straw came when he let a creditor enter our property and take a stove, for collateral, that did not belong to him. He didn't bother to tell us. The other domestic told us, and I had to take Elford to get the stove back. Elford was a very good worker, but we just couldn't trust him. He sold a bicycle three times that wasn't his.

Within a week we had someone at the gate wanting a job. Of course, we are going to be very selective next time we hire a gardener.

It didn't take our last gardener, John, long to gamble all his last pay check away.

Our domestic worker's son has been in the hospital all of this past week. We are not sure when Happy will be back to work. Janet washed the clothes this morning. That is the first time she has had to do it herself for a long time.

28
TRAGEDY AT FAIRVIEW

THE FAMILY WAS *traveling to school with six passengers in the car. The roads were wet, and the car slid in front of a fast traveling vehicle. In this tragic accident Chipo, a fifth grader, was killed instantly. Her sister has a broken hip, and one girl is in a coma, but showing some improvement. Chipo's sister was injured severely and not expected to live. Another student will be in the hospital for at least a month. Still in intensive care is the boy belonging to another family. He had an emergency operation. (Before the parents arrived at the hospital). He had a fractured pelvis, split bladder, and urinary tubes were severed.*

It was a very sad and horrible experience for our parents, our school, and all our church and school families.

Dorothy Forde and I went to the hospital to visit the injured children on that cold Fourth of July. African customs make a week of mourning, which we think is good for their culture. People stay all night to pray and sympathize with the family.

CHIPO'S FUNERAL

Today, eleven-year-old Chipo was buried. We attended the very sad funeral. The church was packed for the funeral. They had two buses plus many cars going to the graveside. The service was LONG! The Fairview students came in uniform to represent our school. They carried the flowers in the church and assisted at the graveside. They do things very differently here. Women carry the casket; I was one of the pallbearers for Chipo.

CONTINUED TAGEDY

A few months later another one of our Fairview School students died.

From what we know his death was not necessarily connected with the accident he was in, which occurred when Chipo died last July. He had an intestine twisted. But the death was caused by neglect. The doctor observed him for three days. What went wrong? The doctor had put off Tapiwa's operation. It was scheduled for that afternoon, the day Tapiwa died. This is no place to get sick. Loraine, Tapiwa's sister, is in my third-grade class.

When someone dies, friends and family go to the person's house and stay for hours. Sometimes all night. They move most of the furniture out of the living room and bring in mattresses. The mother and relatives sit on a mattress or on the floor. The rest of us sit on the carpet. The men sit outside on the veranda. The mother seems to be in shock. There were close to 100 people there to pay their respects. About fifty women at a time are in the living room and about ten in the hall.

> *When someone dies, friends and family go to the person's house and stay for hours. Sometimes all night.*

Feeding the people is hard to figure out. The family is expected to feed all the guests. Also friends bring food. It is hard on poor families. They serve meals, not just snacks. The longer they drag out the mourning period the more food they have to provide. People give donations to help pay expenses. For Tapiwa Munzeiwa's death, over $3,000 was donated to help cover expenses. A letter was sent out to Fairview parents for donations for the family, also. So more would be coming in.

Chipo and Tapiwa are sleeping until Jesus comes, when He will take them to heaven to live with Him forever.

29

RAINS AT LAST

To the people of the arid, southern African nation of Zimbabwe, rain is synonymous with life.

Our domestic worker, Happy, said her SDA church prayed all night for rain after two years of severe drought. The promise God gave to Isaiah was ours. "I will pour water on him who is thirsty, and floods on the dry ground."

When the rains came, and the water rationing was lifted, it made front-page news. Summer rains finally came in November and December. Wonderful to see green trees and grass around town as well as our own yard. We lost several trees and shrubs. We were thankful for our kind neighbor, Ed Russell, who came with his power saw.

Yesterday at church is what they called a "thanksgiving day." It was to give thanks to God for sending rain and ending the drought. Two very good singing groups came to our church in the afternoon. We are always blessed when we hear music in Zimbabwe.

The drought has truly been broken here in Zimbabwe. We have enough water in the dams to last up to eighteen months. If we maintain the present water rationing, I expect that they will double our allotment in a short time.

Of course, we will have to stay on rationing until they build another pipeline to the dams. The pipeline they have now will not carry enough water volume to supply the city water as fast as they can use it.

SCHOOL NEWS ALSO

Last Wednesday it rained for the first time here in months. It was the day our third grade was planning to come to our house and observe the compost pile and make a hay box. Thankfully, God worked it out, and it cleared up, so I brought the children home. The students found and collected a few minibeasts (crickets, praying mantis, ants, and grasshoppers). For the hay box, I had them bring either three carrots, two potatoes, two onions, or celery. We had quite a bit of stew. They peeled and cut up the vegetables and did a great job. Next, we put some hay in the boxes, put the stew in the pot after bringing it to a boil, covered it with more hay and covered the box. We waited until the next day to eat the stew. It really worked. The pot that was sealed the most tasted the best.

FOOD

A MEAL IN ZIMBABWE

Sadza is a staple in Zimbabwe. Sadza is a stiff porridge made from white maize meal. It is garnished with various local vegetables, or meat when available. Fresh vegetables and fruit obtained from the outdoor street market are added to the meal. Trifle, a delicious English dessert pudding finishes the meal.

We buy cloth goods by the meter, milk by the half liter, and vegetables and fruit by kilograms.

Food is plentiful, just not in fast food style. Brown wheat bread is less expensive than white bread. We heard that wheat bread is really white bread with added color. Pasteurized milk is sold by the half liter. Bananas are smaller but sweeter. Other foods are macadamia nuts, oranges, pineapple, mango, strawberries, mulberries, guava, and grapes.

SOY MILK

We made our own soy milk. After soaking soybeans, blend beans with water. Simmer on very low for two or three hours. Pulverize with a blender and strain in a mesh cloth. Don squeezes out the pulp, which DJ gets in his dog food. Add a little honey or another sweetener, chill and enjoy.

We made a spread from chickpeas. We also made our own granola, although the staple breakfast cereal for Zimbabweans is oats.

CREAM CHEESE

Salina is working in the kitchen and putting the lacto into the cheese bag. After it drains twenty-four hours it is like cream cheese. You drain it and strain it in cheese cloth until it dries. Just add a little salt and maybe milk if you want it creamy.

COTTAGE CHEESE

We made some cottage cheese from lacto (buttermilk). All you have to do is heat the lacto for a couple of hours, drain and strain in a cheesecloth until it dries. Add salt and milk and a little lemon juice. Delicious! Cottage cheese and cream cheese are not available here.

30
PASDAD—INDIAN OCEAN EXCURSION

THIS THIRD CONVENTION and continuing education program in Kenya means meetings for me, and a ten-day vacation for Janet.

We are leaving Thursday for Mombasa, Kenya. We will take a plane to Nairobi, then a train to Mombasa. All wives get to go to this conference.

It took four modes of transportation to get us from Zimbabwe to Mombasa, Kenya. Ron Forde drove us to the Bulawayo Airport, then from the plane, we transported to the train in Nairobi, Kenya. After riding all night, we arrived from Nairobi to Mombasa, Kenya. A bus took us to the ferry and the Golden Beach Hotel off the Indian Ocean. We will do the same in reverse going back home. Actually, we could have done without the jerky train ride, but we survived. There are beds (mats) to sleep on. Four to a compartment. A first for us; quite an experience!

Between the Kenya airport and the train station we took to Mombasa, one airport personnel managed to swipe my electric shaver from my suitcase after they had opened and inspected it. Of course, I didn't realize it until later.

Here we are in Kenya at the SDA Dental Convention. Sitting here on the veranda of our hotel, the scenery is lovely; the weather is perfect. The ocean water is warm as is the pool. Even the food is pretty good.

We managed a trip to the city for shopping and a safari excursion to Tsavo Game Park where we saw a cheetah, reticulated giraffe, Grant's gazelle, zebra, eland, elephant, a lioness with three cubs, and many more wild animals.

While Don and Ed are attending classes for continuing education, Linda and I enjoy walking on the beach and seeing the sights. After water aerobics, we will attend a meeting for the dental spouses.

Yesterday Linda and I went out to the reef with Amy, Linda's youngest daughter. We went out in a canoe, the man called it. You have to go when the tide is out. The bottom of the ocean is sure interesting. Lots of different coral, fish, and small animals. We found a few pretty shells and a red starfish. I bought some shells for souvenirs of the Indian Ocean. On the beach, I traded my shoes for a JAMBO (greetings in Swahili) plaque from a man selling carved items.

BRACKENHURST—MORE CONTINUING EDUCATION

The Baptist International Conference Center, held at Brackenhurst, Kenya, thirty miles from Nairobi, Kenya, is an ideal place for our medical-dental convention. Missionaries from all over the world came to attend this continuing education seminar. Doctors, dentists, nurses, dental hygienists, lab technicians, and anyone needing more medical continuing education attended. Ed Russell and I obtained sufficient hours of continuing education to get our dental licenses renewed in the United States. They had Bible study sessions for the ladies. The convention ended with a sacred communion service.

We took time to visit a large tea plantation where tourists are welcome, and we witnessed the tea pickers picking tea. They do pick the tiny little tea leaves.

Several people got sick. We think it was from the water. Thankfully, everyone became well by the time we got ready to go home. While there, Janet took a walk around to see the beauty of the surrounding area. The red flamboyant, purple jacaranda and poor man's orchid bloomed profusely. Some children were on their way to a nearby school. Janet happened to have several pencils with her. You would think she'd given them a hundred dollars they were so delighted. African children appreciate anything you give them, as they are not rich in this world's goods.

31
BETTER LATE THAN NEVER

Shortly before we left to come home, Shirley, my sister, and her husband Ross came for a visit from Oregon just before it was too late. What a great time we had together! Spending Christmas in Wankie Game Park was a surprise for Shirley and Ross and something they had never done before.

Ikhisimusienhle—Merry Christmas!

Boxing day, Whitsunday is the day after Christmas. The tradition is to hand a Christmas box of left-over goodies to the mail carrier, newspaper carrier, or any delivery person.

Christmas isn't as commercialized here, as it is the States. Even the radio stations wait until December before they play Christmas music. Then they play Christmas music only about every other tenth song.

New Year's Eve Ross and Shirley took us to eat at Les Saisons. We came home and had wassail and fruit cake I had made. We saw the New Year in with a game of UpWords. The neighbor's party kept us awake until three a.m. Watching *Anne of Green Gables* shut out the noise. The birds woke us up early the next morning with their familiar songs.

To begin the new year, we swam in the pool and enjoyed visiting. While Don was working Shirley, Ross, and I went shopping for the next few days. We had lots of fun and laughs and spent time buying curios at Bulawayo and Matobo street markets.

Our trip to Matobo Game Park was successful as we saw rhino, zebra, giraffe, and waterbuck among other wild animals. Also, our friends, Ed and Carolyn Mavingera, treated us and Shirley and Ross, to a real African supper at their home. They didn't make us use our fingers to eat as is the custom in Africa.

Tambe and Douglas Mapingerie also invited us to their home for an African dinner.

While visiting one of the campsites, Shirley was sure, while on our walk, she saw a lion on the road. It's certainly possible that she did. Believe me, it didn't take us long to run back to our cabin.

Shirley and Ross enjoyed Chipangali Orphanage, and we took them to tour Solusi University.

Time to leave came all too soon. We took Shirley and Ross to the Bulawayo airport at 7:15 in the morning. God did work it out for them to get home safely.

32
GOING HOME—END OF OUR ONCE-IN-A-LIFETIME JOURNEY

OUR CHURCH FAMILY gave us a going away party. The Golden Spur luncheon was a special going away treat also.

Mavingeres and friends gave us a delicious going away dinner. Saying goodbye to wonderful friends was not easy.

Our missionary friends, Linda, Ed, Dorothy, and Ron, saw us off at the Bulawayo airport. Also, others wished us a safe trip home. Ed, Caroline, their twins, Stephani and Nicole, and Burn Savanda. We boarded Air Zimbabwe, which took us to Frankfort, Germany. On KLM we continued our journey to Atlanta, Georgia, arriving in the United States of America. "Welcome Home" were the words we heard as we checked our baggage through customs at the airport. Realizing we were really home to stay, these words made for teary eyes.

Paula and Pete met us at the airport and drove us to Dad's house. Eventually, we made our rounds to see all the relatives.

WOW! Needless to say, it was good to be home. Yes, the experience of a lifetime and GOD DID WORK IT OUT.

When we arrived home, the General Conference sent us a book, *Re-Entry. Making The Transition From Missions To Life At Home*, by Peter Jordan.

Things we learned: We learned that you can live with a simple diet, without the hustle and bustle, and without many of our modern conveniences. We learned that African people are friendly, respectful, quiet-natured, and were wonderful to work with. The African people we associated with were very spiritual and enthusiastic about serving Jesus and witnessing to others. We expect to see many of our African friends in heaven someday soon.

MOVING ON—to our next missionary encounter—TRINIDAD, WEST INDIES

But that's another story!

33
REMEMBERING ZIMBABWE

Thinking over the past seven and a half years
We've enjoyed all you people, and our careers.
Never have we regretted our move to your city
Even though times of drought weren't very pretty
The long queues for bread and white mealie meal
Certainly made many get a raw deal.
Five days here brought us our initiation
Thieves used our windows to steal our possessions
But burglar bars, domestic help, and big dog, DJ,
Put an end to our worry; the thieves stayed away.
We'll remember your game parks, Great Ruins, and Vic Falls
History museum, African games, socials in Advent Hall.
Women's retreats, evangelistic meetings, Fairview School,
Baptisms by the hundreds in BASS swimming pool.
Potluck at Hillside, the early-teenagers,
Beautiful singing from groups of all ages.
Jackarandas, flamboyant, giant poinsettias we see,
Heuglin's robins, grey louries, guinea fowl so free.
Egyptian and spitting cobras, right in our yard,
Green mamba, too; had to be on our guard.
Elephants, giraffes, baboons, and kudu,
Rhinos, leopards, and hippopotamuses, too.

Emergency taxies, robots, buses overflowing,
Breakdown, and accidents with Quicks a-towing.
Ndebele course, my certificate I got,
Can I speak the language? Guess it wasn't my lot.
At the Adventist Dental Practice Don couldn't have found
Better working conditions with Ron, Ken, and Ed round.
I'll always remember my wonderful students
Who kept my days full of fun and prudence.
Blind beggars, street people, vegetable vendors,
The markets in town for all the big spenders.
Remember our pastors, Pierson, Machazi, and Lea?
Pastor Rhoades, too, "Church, are you with me?"
All Bulawayo churches filled to the brim,
While various preachers bring us closer to Him.
Jesus will come before very long.
How can He wait? Things on earth are all wrong.
Not as He planned it; sorrow, sickness, and strife;
He wants us home, He's promised eternal life.
We'll think of you often and pray for you, too,
See you in heaven and on the earth made new.

GLOSSARY

baby marrow—zucchini squash

bush—wide open spaces, mainly unpopulated areas of Africa

chalet—six-sided structure with pointed roof.

colour—color

coloured—mixture of black and white races

biscuits—cookies

queue—waiting lines

nappies—diapers

expatriate—a person residing in a country other than his native country

finished—done, over, complete

groundnuts—peanuts

Harare—capitol of Zimbabwe

kopje—hill

kya—domestic house in Zimbabwe

knob carrier—club with knob on top, made with very heavy wood

lay by—rest stop

madam—what the hired help call Janet

maize—corn

masta—what the hired help call Don

mealies—a pudding or bread both made with ground corn

Ndebele—ethnic group making up about 15 percent of Zimbabwe's population

suicide month—October; very hot

paw paw—papaya

PR—permanent return

robots—traffic lights

sadza—main staple made from white corn

Shona—ethnic group in Zimbabwe, which makes up about 80 percent of the population

TIA—this is Africa

zed—Z

NEWS FROM HOME

Daughter, Karen, a baby girl, born on Don's birthday.

Paula called and said she and Pete got married in Jamaica.

Gifts from home—flowers sent.

Don's parents moved closer to conveniences of store and church.

Daughter Beth is coming to visit.

Mother broke her hip and had a plastic hip socket replacement.

Mother is planning her trip to come back with us from our furlough.

Niece Reda is getting married to Chris Davis.

Sister Shirley and Ross got married.

Daughter Linda has a new husband, moved to NY from Texas.

Niece Melody graduated with RN in NY.

Nephew Keith and Malissa had baby boy, Tommy 7 lb. 4 oz., red hair.

Niece Sunshine received nursing degree.

Nephew Philip injured in a motorcycle accident.

Nephew Ernie and wife had baby.

Philip married, has a wife.

Debbie sent a beautiful bouquet of flowers for Mother's Day.

A tornado struck our home state, Huntsville, AL.

Niece Terri Lee, a paramedic, died.

Granddaughter Alicia's jump roping team won first place in statewide competition.

TEACH Services, Inc.
P U B L I S H I N G
www.TEACHServices.com • (800) 367-1844

We invite you to view the complete
selection of titles we publish at:
www.TEACHServices.com

We encourage you to write us
with your thoughts about this,
or any other book we publish at:
info@TEACHServices.com

TEACH Services' titles may be purchased in
bulk quantities for educational, fund-raising,
business, or promotional use.
bulksales@TEACHServices.com

Finally, if you are interested in seeing
your own book in print, please contact us at:
publishing@TEACHServices.com
We are happy to review your manuscript at no charge.

CPSIA information can be obtained
at www.ICGtesting.com
Printed in the USA
JSHW051209090621
15696JS00006B/119